Best Poems of 1974
Borestone Mountain Poetry Awards 1975

A Compilation of Original Poetry
Published in Magazines of the
English-Speaking World in 1974

Volume 27

Pacific Books, Publishers, Palo Alto, California
1975

International Standard Book Number 0-87015-219-X.
Library of Congress Catalog Card Number 49-49262.
Printed and bound in the United States of America.

PACIFIC BOOKS, PUBLISHERS
P.O. Box 558, Palo Alto, California 94302

FOREWORD

Best Poems of 1974 presents the Borestone Mountain Poetry Awards' twenty-seventh annual selections of poems from magazines of the English-speaking world issued in 1974. The poems in approximately one hundred and fifty magazines are read by the reading staff. Poems are not accepted directly from the poets. A poem is eligible if it is a first printing appearing in the year of the selections and is not over one hundred lines. Reprints, translations, and unpublished poems are not considered. Thus some three hundred poems are selected. When the year's selections are complete, copies of the poems are sent to the judges with the names of the authors and magazines deleted, as there is no intention of recognizing established names in preference to newcomers or apportioning selections between magazines and countries.

The judges score their top seventy-five individual preferences and forward the results to the office of the Managing Editor, where a tabulation of the scores determines the final selections. The three highest scores are the winners of the year's cash awards. Because of the anonymity preserved during the selection process, the final results may include more than one poem by a poet and a number of poems from the same periodical. This editorial procedure and the rules for selecting a poem have been consistent throughout the twenty-seven volumes.

Borestone Mountain Poetry Awards, which was established nearly thirty years ago, is supported by a non-profit literary foundation by the same name. The purpose is to preserve in book form each year some of the poems of merit that otherwise would be lost among countless magazine pages. The twenty-seven annual volumes have presented 2,063 poems by more than 1,000 poets, and the series now serves as an easy and useful reference to some of the best writing in contemporary poetry during the past three decades.

"Fox" by Michael Dennis Browne received the first award of $300. "Ten Years and More" by Miriam Waddington won the second award of $200. "Beauty and the Beast" by David Wagoner received the third award of $100.

The editors gratefully acknowledge permission to reprint these selected poems from the magazines, publishers, and authors owning the copyrights. The Contents lists the magazine and issue in 1974 from which the selection was made. At the time the selections were completed in March 1975, some poems were scheduled for reprinting in collections of the poets. These subsequent printings and other recognitions are recorded under "Acknowledgments and Notes."

THE EDITORS

HOWARD SERGEANT
  British Commonwealth
  Magazines
  (except Canada)

WADDELL AUSTIN
  Managing Editor

HILDEGARDE FLANNER

FRANCES MINTURN HOWARD

GEMMA D'AURIA

GARY MIRANDA

ACKNOWLEDGMENTS AND NOTES

"William Blackburn, Riding Westward" by James Applewhite was first published in the *Sewanee Review* 82 (Winter 1974) and copyrighted © 1974 by the University of the South. It is reprinted by permission of the editor. The poem has been subsequently included in Mr. Applewhite's first collection of poems, *Statues of the Grass*, published by the University of Georgia Press and is reprinted by permission of the Press and the author.

"What I Wanted To Say" by Stephen Berg, which was selected from the April 1974 issue of *The American Review*, will be included in his collection of poems, *Grief*, to be published by Grossman Publishers, New York, in October 1975.

"The Bitch Madonna" by Peter Bland was selected from the magazine *Islands, The New Zealand Quarterly of Arts and Letters*, Vol. 3, No. 2, Winter 1974, 4 Sealy Road, Torbay, Auckland 10, New Zealand.

"Next Love" by David Bromige is reprinted by permission from *The Hudson Review*, Vol. XXVI, No. 4, Winter 1973-74, copyright © 1973 by The Hudson Review, Inc.

"Of Dancing" by Alan Brownjohn is to be included in his new collection of poems, *A Song of Good Life*, to be published by Secker and Warburg Ltd., London, in October 1975.

"The Sun Helmet" by Charles Edward Eaton is reprinted from *Shenandoah, The Washington and Lee University Review*, copyright © 1974 with permission of the Editor. The poem will be included in Mr. Eaton's sixth collection, *The Man in the Green Chair*, which won the work-in-progress, Alice Fay di Castagnola Award of $3,500 in the spring of 1974.

"Love on the Underground" by D. J. Enright is included in his collection, *Sad Ires*, to be published by Chatto and Windus Ltd., London, in October 1975.

"The Museum: The Prison: The Madhouse" by Kathy Epling is reprinted from *Prairie Schooner*, copyright © 1973 by The University of Nebraska Press.

"Let This Cup Keep" by Norma Farber is reprinted by permission from *The Christian Science Monitor*, copyright © 1974 The Christian Science Publishing Society. All rights reserved.

CONTENTS

Michael Dennis Browne: (*First Award*)   Fox   1
The New Yorker—August 19

Miriam Waddington: (*Second Award*) Ten Years and More   4
The Tamarack Review—No. 62

David Wagoner: (*Third Award*)   Beauty and the Beast   6
The Western Humanities Review—Summer

Jonathan Aaron: Going Away   9
The American Review—October

Virginia H. Adair: Drowned Girl   11
Poet Lore—Spring

James Applewhite: William Blackburn, Riding Westward   12
The Sewanee Review—Winter

Kenneth Arnold: Bonebag   14
Poetry Northwest—Spring

Roy Bennett: Respected Citizens, True Democrats   15
Outposts (England)—Winter

Stephen Berg: What I Wanted To Say   16
The American Review—April

Wendell Berry: The Bed   17
The Virginia Quarterly Review—Summer

Wendell Berry: A Purification   20
The Southern Review—Autumn

Raymond Biasotti: Hektor   21
The Beloit Poetry Journal—Spring

Peter Bland: The Bitch Madonna   24
Islands (New Zealand)—Winter

David Bromige: Next Love   26
The Hudson Review—Winter 73/74

T. Alan Broughton: "Hold, Hold"   27
The Virginia Quarterly Review—Summer

Alan Brownjohn: Of Dancing   29
Critical Quarterly (England)—Summer

Jean Burden: In Other People's Houses   32
Chicago Tribune Magazine—June 30

Charles Causley: Silent Jack   33
The Times Literary Supplement (England)—March 15

Jim Ciletti:	Lady	35
	Poet Lore—Winter, Vol. 69, No. 4	
Wayne Dodd:	In Athens, Ohio	38
	The Southern Review—Winter	
Ruth Doty:	The Maskmaker	40
	Chicago Review—Vol. 25, No. 4	
Charles Edward Eaton:	The Giraffe	43
	Southwest Review—Summer	
Charles Edward Eaton:	The Sun Helmet	44
	Shenandoah—Fall	
D. J. Enright:	Love on the Underground	45
	The Listener (England)—February	
Kathy Epling:	The Museum: The Prison: The Madhouse	46
	Prairie Schooner—Winter 1973-74	
Nissim Ezekiel:	Why the English Lessons Ended	47
	Outposts (England)—Spring	
Norma Farber:	Let This Cup Keep	49
	The Christian Science Monitor—Nov. 8	
Norma Farber:	The Way Shadows Refuse	50
	Poetry Northwest—Spring	
James Fenton:	Prison Island	51
	The Times Literary Supplement (England)—June	
Diane Elizabeth Fry:	Twenty Years of Hearing Jack	53
	Quarry (Canada)—Summer	
Brendan Galvin:	The Bats	54
	The New Yorker—July 8	
Louise Glück:	The Drowned Children	56
	The New Yorker—November 25	
Daniel Halpern:	The Lady Knife-Thrower	57
	The New Yorker—May 27	
Gwen Harwood:	Carnal Knowledge II	58
	Poetry Australia (Australia)—No. 50	
Raymond Henri:	Grave	60
	Chicago Tribune Magazine—April 14	
William Heyen:	This Father of Mine	61
	The Georgia Review—Fall	
David Holbrook:	A Thin Time	65
	The Listener (England)—March	

John Hollander:	Burning Leaves	67
	The American Review—January	
Ora May Hull:	In the Moon-Backed Morning	69
	Poet Lore—Spring	
Anne Hussey:	Cinderella Liberated	71
	The New Yorker—August 19	
Carolyn Kizer:	October, 1973	72
	The American Review—April	
Susu Knight:	Icarus Flying	74
	Poet Lore—Winter	
Calvin Lapp:	Emblem	75
	The Fiddlehead (Canada)—Winter	
Philip Legler:	Sheet Monger, Blanket Hoarder	76
	The Paris Review—Summer	
Lawrence Mathews:	Reunion	78
	The Canadian Forum (Canada)—September	
William Matthews:	In Memory of W. H. Auden	80
	The Atlantic Monthly—October	
Eric Millward:	I Think My Mother Never Knew	82
	Outposts (England)—Spring	
Herbert Morris:	Being a Soldier (Forest Hills)	83
	The American Review—April	
Herbert Morris:	The Disappearance	85
	Kayak—June	
Sheila B. Nickerson:	Departure	88
	Quarry (Canada)—Spring	
Leslie Norris:	Barn Owl	89
	Poetry Northwest—Spring	
Ilmars Purens:	The Graverobbers' Children	91
	The Minnesota Review—Spring/Fall	
Anne Ridler:	Free Fall	93
	Critical Quarterly (England)—Spring	
Ralph Robin:	Silence and Speech	95
	The Virginia Quarterly Review—Spring	
William Pitt Root:	Year of the Monkey	97
	Northwest Review—Vol. XIV, No. 2	
Gibbons Ruark: Talking Myself to Sleep in the Mountains		100
	The New Yorker—September 23	

Ira Sadoff: Love Poem   101
                              Poetry Northwest—Summer
Aram Saroyan: Madness   102
                                The Paris Review—Fall
Barbara Saunders: Because   104
                           The Fiddlehead (Canada)—Spring
Michael Schmidt: In the Air   105
                              The Hudson Review—Summer
Gjertrud Schnackenberg: Letter from Brooklyn   106
                           The Beloit Poetry Journal—Summer
Margaret Scott:
      Stories of My Mother's Childhood, Told in Wartime   107
                              Quadrant (Australia)—April
Carol Shields: Mother   108
                           The Fiddlehead (Canada)—Winter
Carol Shields: Service Call   109
                           The Fiddlehead (Canada)—Winter
Clarice Short: The Owl on the Aerial   110
                        The Western Humanities Review—Winter
John Stone: He Makes a House Call   111
                   Southern Poetry Review—Fall Vol. XIV, No. 2
Constance Urdang: Exorcism   113
                                   Yankee—February
Cory Wade: Transformations   114
                                   Poetry—December
David Wagoner: The Lesson   115
                              The New Yorker—April 22
David Wagoner: Living in the Ruins   117
                                     Poetry—June
David Wagoner: Talking to Barr Creek   118
                              The Hudson Review—Spring
Ted Walker: Vipers,   119
                              The New Yorker—November 11
Tom Wayman: The Unemployment Insurance
                        Commission Poems: 1. The Nationalist   121
                           The Canadian Forum (Canada)—April
Robert Lewis Weeks: Softshoe   124
                              Prairie Schooner—Spring

Best   Poems of 1974

FOX

Driving fast down the country roads.
To a committee. A class.
When I stop for gas, a highway patrolman tells me
one of my lights is out.
Then he drives off to take up his position
behind a bush at the bottom of the hill
to wait for speeders.

Yesterday, a snake, black & green, coiled
down by the railroad tracks.
His mouth bloody, he moved slowly,
he looked like he was dying.
Boats being pulled up out of the water.
The dog ran into the lake
after the sticks the children threw,
and stood looking back at me from the gold water.

On TV, the faces of the captured Israeli pilots.
Syrian film of Israeli planes crashing,
martial music. The patrolman crouched behind the bush,
the mouth of the snake, hard & red,
his green-black body without ease,
a bent stick by him, as if maybe
a child had beaten him with it, maybe the same
child throwing sticks to the dog in the water.

Hurrying through Wisconsin.
Hundreds of black birds tossed up
from a cornfield, turning away. Arab or Israeli?
The man in the parked patrol car,
the sticks rushing, failing through the air.
County Road Q, County Road E.
The committee meeting, waiting for me.

The fox! It is a fox! It is a red fox!
I slow up. He is in the road.
I slow. He moves into the grass, but not far.
He doesn't seem that afraid.
Look, look! I say to the white dog behind me.
Look, Snow Dog, a fox! He doesn't see him.
And this fox. What he does now is
go a little further, & turn, & look at me.
I am braked, with the engine running, looking at him.

I say to him, Fox—you Israeli or Arab?
You are red; whose color is that?
Was it you brought blood
to the mouth of the snake? The patrolman
is waiting, the dog standing
in the gold water. Would you
run fetch, what would you
say to my students? He looks at me.

And I say, So go off, leave us, over
the edge of that hill, where we shan't see you.
Go on—as the white she-wolf can't,
who goes up & down, up & down
against her bars all day,
all night maybe.

Be fox for all of us, those in zoos,
in classrooms, those on committees,
neither Assistant Fox nor Associate Fox
but Full Fox, fox with tenure, runner
on any land, owner of nothing, anywhere,
fox beyond all farmers,
fox neither Israeli nor Arab,
fox the color of the fall & the hill.

And you, O fellow with my face,
do this for me: one day
come back to me, to my door,
show me my own crueller face, my face
as it really cruelly is, beyond what

a committee brings out in me, or the woman
I love when I have to leave her.
But no human hand, fox untouched, fox
among the apples & barns, O call out
in your own fox-voice through the air over Wisconsin
that is full of the falling
Arab & Israeli leaves, red, red,
locked together, falling, in spirals, burning . . .

be a realler, cleaner thing,
no snake with a broken body, no bent stick,
no patrolman crouched behind a bush
with bloody mouth, no stick thrown,
no beloved tamed dog in the water . . .

And let us pull up now out of the water
the boats, & call the leaves home
down out of the air, Arab or Israeli;
& you, my real red fox in Wisconsin,
as I let out the clutch & leave you,
you come back that time, be cruel then,
teach me your fox-stink even, more than now, as I
hurry, kind & fragrant, into committee,
& the leaves falling, red, red.
And the fox runs on.

Michael Dennis Browne

TEN YEARS AND MORE

When my husband
lay dying, a mountain
a lake, three
cities, ten years
and more
lay between us:

There were our
sons, my wounds
and theirs,
despair, loneliness,
handfuls of un-
hammered nails
pictures never
hung all

The uneaten
meals and unslept
sleep; there was
retirement, and
worst of all
a green umbrella
he can never
take back.

I wrote him a
letter but all
I could think of
to say was: do you
remember Severn
River, the red canoe
with the sail
and lee-boards?

I was really saying
for the sake of our
youth and our love
I forgave him for
everything
and I was asking him
to forgive me too.

MIRIAM WADDINGTON

BEAUTY AND THE BEAST

Men wept when they saw her breasts, squinted with pain
At her clear profile, boggled at her knees,
Turned slack-jawed at her rear-view walking away,
And every available inch of her hair and skin
Had been touched by love poems and delicious gossip.
The most jaundiced and jaded people in the village
Agreed with the Prince: young Beauty was a beauty.

But through the long day he doused and plucked his roses,
Drained and refilled his moat, or caulked his dungeons,
And all night long he clocked the erring planets,
Pondered the lives of saints like a Latin-monger,
Or sat up half-seas over with sick falcons,
While Beauty lingered in her sheerest nightgowns
With the light behind her, wilting from sheer boredom.

"You're a bore!" she said. "Prince Charming is a bore!"
She cried to the gaping seamstresses and fishwives.
"He's a bore!" she yelled to the scullions and butcher's helpers.
"That tedious, bland, preoccupied, prickling Princeling
Is a bore's bore!" she told the bloody barbers
And waxy chandlers leaning out to watch her
Dragging her rear-view home to Mother and Father.

But deep in the woods, behind a bush, the Beast
Had big ideas about her. When she slipped by,
Hiking her skirts to give her legs free sway
And trailing a lovely, savage, faint aroma
Fit to unman a beast, the Beast said, "Beauty,
Come live with me in the bushes where it's chancy,
Where it's scare and scare alike, where it's quick and murky."

She looked him over. Though the light was patchy,
She could see him better than she wanted to:
Wherever men have skin, the Beast had hair;
Wherever men have hair, he had black bristles;
Wherever men have bristles, he grew teeth;
And wherever men have teeth, his snaggling tusks
Lapped over his smile. So Beauty said, "No thank you."

"You'd be a sweet relief. I'd gorge on you.
I'm sick of retching my time with hags and gorgons.
You're gorgeous. Put down my rising gorge forever."
She remembered her mother whispering: *The Beast
Is a bargain. It's a well-known fact that, later,
He turns into a Prince, humble and handsome,
With unlimited credit and your father's mustache.*

*So all you have to do is grin and bear him
Till the worst is over.* But Beauty felt uncertain.
Still, after the Prince, it seemed like now or never,
And maybe all men were monsters when they saw her,
And maybe the ugliest would teach her sooner.
Her heart felt colder than a wizard's whistle:
She said, "Poor Beast, how can I say I love you?"

With horny fingers caressing everything
Available on the little world of her body,
The Beast then took her gently, his rich odor
Wafting about them like the mist from graveyards,
And Beauty began to branch out like a castle
Taller than trees, and from the highest tower
She loosened her long hair, and the Beast climbed it.

When he was spent, he lay beside her, brushing
Leaves from her buttresses, and said, "I love you."
She shrank back to herself and felt afraid.
"You'll change into something much more comfortable
Now that you've taken me," she said. "I know:
You'll be transformed to someone like Prince Charming."
"I'm always like this," he said, and drooled a little.

"If you're going to change, change now," she told him, weeping.
"Peel off that monster suit and get it over."
"I wear myself out, not in," he said. "I'll love you
In all the worst ways, as clumsily as heaven."
"Thank God," she said. And Beauty and the Beast
Stole off together, arm in hairy arm,
And made themselves scarce in the bewitching forest.

DAVID WAGONER

GOING AWAY

She seemed to be waiting
for an imaginary visit,
or for a signal or a message
telling her to move, perhaps
for good. She had a look
which said her life
was neither here nor there,
but where I'd never dream
of finding it.
What had happened?   What would?
We had only to wish it, and it did
in the countryside we drove through,
where the houses all exploded
softly, as if doing so
ten years before in a theater,
or in time with the histories
of neighbors who had arrived
from Germany.   At night
in the mirror, we saw our faces
ripple and break apart
in flurries of light, then fall
back into the darkness they had left
with such difficulty.
Making love blindfolded, our breath
like paper being torn, was what
we had left after everything else
had been taken away.
I know what you mean, she said,
but it was never me.
What we were looking for was that

particular instant of being someone else
before politeness, kindness,
or even the hope of love
takes over, a moment
we could recognize when it happened,
but which we could never anticipate
or recall.   Both of us
must have believed, say, in music
or voices from a house we stopped
to watch some afternoon
as clear and cool as the lessons
it could have concealed.
But neither of us doubted
that year by year the body
fills with annulled stars,
that the word you trust is always
ready to change sides, to enter
the heart like a blade you can't see
until it has happened.
I know what you mean,
but the woman in this picture
keeps a balance I'd never stand for.
Besides, the shadow of a branch
has cut her face in half.
Further talk of places
we had been, not very interesting
places, where the good thing was
you didn't have to speak
the language.   And afterwards,
sending each other telegrams.
Here I am at last, hers read.
The buildings are whiter
than I imagined. Mine read
essentially the same.

JONATHON AARON

DROWNED GIRL

Face the drowned girl, whose fighting limbs and breath
the profound wave silenced with dear images:

Look, here's the first round world, equipped with warmth
and a wise nipple knowing your needs. See next
a million children hard at play; your feet
the fastest, your fist triumphant, your fingers thieving
bright apples from their counterpoint of leaves.

See here, said the wave, and urged her dreaming body
down surging stairs of gloom deepward, I divulge
the bee-stretched flower, the honey winging home
a singing dot in the pure silences.

And so, corrupted by the dear story, her heart
gave over its rhythm to the sea's monody. She gave
her white body for a chord in the dirge of herself
and twice reclimbed the cloudy stair for ecstasy
of slow descent through failures and desires.

No push of pulse, no battle in the blood
finally disturbed the saline melody
when last the swell through dissonance of surf
bore her, loose-fingered and with heavy hair;
to resolution on the empty shore.

O listen for the notes, the last white chord
struck trailing on the sand, before it brings
the curious and the screams; face the drowned girl
before the blanket comes, and the grave men.

VIRGINIA H. ADAIR

WILLIAM BLACKBURN, RIDING WESTWARD

Here in this mild, Septembral December, you have died.
Leaves from the black oaks litter our campus walks,
Where students move, or stand and talk, not knowing
Your wisdom's stature, illiterate in the book of your face.

So often we walked along the old stone wall at night,
Looked up at your window, where lamplight cleft your brow,
And knew you were suffering for us the thornier passages,
Transfixed by *Lear*, or staring ahead to the heart
Of Conrad's Africa.   Sometimes we ventured inside,
To be welcomed by an excellent whiskey, Mozart's *Requiem*.
This clarity of music and ice revealed once in air
A poem as you read it: as Vaughan created "The World,"
Eternity's ring shining "calm as it was bright."

On a wall was the picture of you riding on a donkey,
Caught in mid-pilgrimage, to a holy land I do not remember.
But your missionary parents had borne you in Persia,
And after we'd learned that we saw you as explorer;
From hometowns scattered on an American map marked
Terra incognita for the heart, you led treks
Into our inward countries, and still seem discovering before,
Through straits to "the Pacific Sea," or the "Eastern riches."

Left on these New World shores—so thoroughly possessed,
So waiting to be known—on all sides round we see
Great trees felled and lying, their bodies disjointed,
Or standing in all weather, broken, invaded by decay.

The worn landscape of your features, the shadows
Days had cast under eyes, were part of the night
That steadily encroaches on the eastward globe, as it rotates
In sunlight.   Out of your age shone a gleam of youth,
Which seems with cedars' searing to sing in the forest
In wolf's ears of green flame.

                                        Still, you are dead.
Your system is subject to entropy.   Cells' change
Reduced your monarchical features to a kingship of chaos.
"With faltering speech, and visage incomposed,"
You said good night, between pangs of the withering hunger
Which filled your dying dreams with apples and cheeses.

In spite of the revolt of your closest ally, your body,
You died with the nobility you'd taught, and teaching, learned.
And now you roam my brain, King Lear after death.
The broken girl in your arms is only your spirit,
A poor fool hanged by Cordelia, by the straits of fever.

We visit your old office on campus in grief.
Outside, trees lift winterward branches toward
A sky in chaos.   The patterning which spins the stars
Exists outside this weather we live under.

We see only branches against those clouds' inclemency.

                                        JAMES APPLEWHITE

BONEBAG

These are not my bones in a dry spring,
 but I collect them gently
 so that they will not break more
 than they have

and carry them back to town with me:
 they have teeth and polish:
 a wilderness grows out of them,
 sprawled womanly

on the hills I move through, my own bones
 secure in the bag of my body.
 These bones curve with pleasure
 to touch this piece

to that and so on: intricacy now gone.
 Here this sturdy legbone
 tongued and grooved for that snug
 socket of hip:

but the severed spine twists in a semblance
 of agony among the small
 washed pieces of body left over after
 its violence,

the jaw still hinged delicate to the skull
 which is whole and amazed
 with slopes and depressions, windows
 on to nowhere.

I cannot tell the name of this animal nor
 how it came to die here,
 but I know I don't want to end like
 this, broken.

KENNETH ARNOLD

RESPECTED CITIZENS, TRUE DEMOCRATS

Sowerberry & Son, Undertakers
Shines gold through the frosted parlour window on
Waxed oak panels and sheathed arum lilies.
Death's their stock-in-trade. They're long inured.
Top End, Bottom End: it's all the same.
The grief, the new black clothes (so photogenic),
Mostly a show for neighbours or High Street.
They act a sort of eunuchs at an orgy.

Theirs is a learned and calculated tact.
The old man knows to a pinch how much to take,
From whom, and when. And Son (who looks no younger)
No less. The wrinkles of their mystery,
To make the dead presentable with rouge
And wadding, lie scored in the rough-cut pineboard masks
They view the world through, and their wives. Beneath
Their enormous tread worms chuckle in the ground.

Their hatbands shine like grease as they step out,
Breathing raw brandy with the next-of-kin.
For Sowerberry, plumes, the horse parade
With the glass-walled hearse to impress the Rotary
And add that touch of class. Son prefers
The motorised cortege, the incinerator,
Piped musak—less fuss. That's no good.
Automation's death to a decent trade.

ROY BENNETT

WHAT I WANTED TO SAY

I woke at six. Birds cried from the roofs.
No sun yet, a gray sky and clouds,
the first cars taking men to work. I slept
downstairs on the couch, half the night
I saw your emptied face, your weak shiny hands
that had lost their warmth after the heart attack.
Like water. You could barely talk. I thought
about what we say to each other even now,
and about the white fires of the crematory
furnace that made you ashes in a box.
All this came up as easily as the wind
shakes the leaves on one of the trees outside my house
then stops, and the leaves hang there, so quiet
you believe something miraculous will happen.
The streetlamps glow with a sudden brightness,
you feel satisfied with the cracked chimneys,
the dull yellow haze blowing across the stars,
you could sit endlessly on the steps, smoking,
doing nothing, and never speak again.
But this isn't what I wanted to say.
The birds were calling me, I think. Or someone.
There were tears. I stumbled. My jaws hurt.
I bent over my sleeping children to say good-bye
and each one turned to me and smiled. But this
came back—your dead face was a blank
white flower opening in me, which I couldn't touch.
I stood somewhere, saying, "Nobody can say this."

STEPHEN BERG

THE BED

1

Crumbs of rotten stone,
shards of bone, the leavings
and the ruins of lives—
the ground's a grave, and so
it thrives. Another day,
another day, sing
the sleepers in their bed.
Under the bitter ice,
among the overthrown
stems that bore them, are hid
the seeds, in whose silence
the future and the past
internested lie,
two lovers in their sleep.
A thousand thousand years
will bloom here in the spring,
upon the living sing
the blessing of the dead.

2

As though I stood, unaware,
on a great bed, and one of the sleepers
turned, making the footing
uneasy, I see them:
a part of hunters by a low fire,
two men and a boy;
a third man, wounded, lies still,
his body already given
to what is beyond the light.
His eyes follow the movements
of the other men, and rest again
upon the boy. His breaths are loud
in the surrounding quiet.
The fire is cupped in a hollow
of the ground. Behind them
the bluff offers a defense.
They keep their weapons in their hands.

The wounded man cumbering them like a limp,
they have left their pursuers
how far behind they do not know, crossed the river,
climbed here to the valley's rim
to rest, and to ease this death.
Their custom is to bury on these heights.

They speak in sentences I hear the music of
but do not know, and again
are silent in the way of hunters at night,
or in the way of the hunted
who know the ways of the hunters,
listening to what may be coming up
under the wind. Listening
to the distance, they sit in a golden cave
of October leaves, the light
around them restless among the trees.

The man is dead in his stillness
for the time of three breaths
before they notice, or before they move.
Digging with sticks and hands, they scoop
a grave in the valley's lip,
lay him in, cover him, cover earth and rock with leaves,
tramp the fire, spread leaves over the ash
by touch. The place again
is as it was, night filling it.

And they are swiftly on their way,
their steps silent
on the damp leaves. They are gone
as long as the fate of men is
to be gone from the places they have been.

The leaves of the years
fall, and the rains.
Burrow, frost, and root thrust
in the mold. Gravity
gathers the occasions
of an implacable healing.
The dead one has turned
to the light again,
the valley wider by his body's width.

3
Like the fields, my mind's a bed.
Graves open in my head.

The dead rise and walk about
The timeless fields of thought.

I am by right of birth their own.
I mark like briefly lettered stone

Their beds, and I sing
Their powerful sleep, the opening

By which, nameless or named, they must
Empower and stir again this dust.

To sorrow, their death is long.
Their coming again is song.

WENDELL BERRY

A PURIFICATION

At start of spring I open a trench
in the ground. I put into it
the winter's accumulation of paper,
pages I do not want to read
again, useless words, fragments,
errors. And I put into it
the contents of the outhouse:
light of the sun, growth of the ground,
finished with one of their journeys.
To the sky, to the wind, then,
and to the faithful trees, I confess
my sins: that I have not been happy
enough, considering my good fortune;
that I have listened to too much noise;
that I have been inattentive to wonders;
that I have lusted after praise.
And then upon the gathered refuse
of mind and body, I close the trench,
folding shut again the dark,
the deathless earth. Beneath that seal
the old escapes into the new.

WENDELL BERRY

HEKTOR

From the top of the wall, your father yells,
The others are watching. Your mother screams.

Achilles is streaking across the field.
His horses are white with sweat.
The seizing axles smoke and howl.
But even worse, Athena, whom you can't see
rides beside him and their hairs mingle.

The Grey-eyed Daughter of God, Hektor,
flies with Achilles toward your city.

Throw your spear, pull the long bronze sword,
throw the temples, none of it will help you.
You were dead when Athena touched her
    father's arm,
when he knew that shiver he dare not name.

Before this day is out
you will know the distance of your city.
Your white-handed throat will beat like a heart
as awful Achilles comes whirling and sneering
hulking your army across his knees.
You will strip your priceless armor
and crawl backward to your mother.
You will drag by your feet from Achilles' car.
You will plead for your life
and your wall-bound, stomping men will hear;
and all the poets will strike your name
from the pages of their singing books.

It is so, Hektor.

For even now your courage fails
as History coils around you rattling.

Even now the white-eyed terror of horses
rolls you out from your name-walled room
as twice-crossed Achilles arches toward you
end over end through the scattering faces.

And you come to realize how you, too,
will bite the strings that rise from your hands
straight-tight into the buzzing afternoon,
the gaudy silver wires of your orchid life.

But even worse, Hektor,
when this auburn-eyed Achilles
comes broad against the hunting sun,
you will find that you love him,
and your muscled arms will forfeit
the warlocked falcon of your pride.

And that's what will destroy you.
and that's what will send you running
round the disbelief of your watching town,
caterwauling, as bridge-falling Death
closes upon you sectioning this field
with the hand made measures of Time.

Raise your pitiful stick
bellow and curse, but look
look how the afternoon bends
as something comes you cannot see.

It is not Achilles
(though it is Achilles)
It is not even Death
(though it is Death)
look how even Athena
and her proud father
scurry away, somersaulting,

for behind them the air trembles
hits itself like a deaf mute to speak
as man-breaking Time, that has no equal,
rolls appointed on its sky-wide wheels.

But all you can see is Achilles,
tail-gating Achilles; and so for you

Goddamned Hektor, Panting Hektor,
cast the one good perfect spear
the only accomplishment of your life.
Throw it soldier, at the afternoon.
See how it flies as it was made
perfectly straight and kills the ground.

Inside you now an eight year old boy
charges the flowers with wooden sword.
Charging Achilles, Athena and Zeus;
Charging the thing that stands aloof
that doesn't move, that moves, and doesn't
    move.

Do it Hektor; even in this hopelessness.
Lower your head and charge the afternoon.
It is right and proper that you should.

RAYMOND BIASOTTI

THE BITCH MADONNA

In Tiepolo's
Woman Taken in Adultery
Christ kneels
before this magnificent tart
and looks
at Peter—who as usual
wants to punch
some hypocrite on the nose.

That look's a warning.
She's hot stuff. Don't blow it!
With her around
someone has to throw stones.
She laughs
at all this libido showing
and stands
tit-proud. One bare shoulder

daring anyone
to bruise *that* body. This mob
—you can bet your bricks—
once offered other gifts. She
knows these well-heeled yobos
intimately. Christ kneels. . . .
She probably thinks he's queer.
She prefers the fisherman

he's holding back
with one mild-mannered glance.
Her look is harder . . .
begging no one's pardon. After all
it was always her job to bring
these bully-boys to the boil.
She enjoys
watching the middle-classes rage

as they try to disown
their dirty washing. Christ kneels—
a mirror to the mob's deceit.
They stare back . . . eyes
like broken bottles.
Tiepolo ejaculates on to his brush . . .
body-colour
for his bitch madonna.

PETER BLAND

NEXT LOVE

The heat put it in my mind
I guess, so when I saw that glow
on the horizon eastward, growing
while I watched, the prairie
all around me dry, ready for fire

my excitement told me
this was what I saw, burning
everywhere, fixed
by the wonder for five minutes
when I thought about it later, when I thought
to run back to the house & let them know

there was something someone ought to cope with,
somehow.   Before I could the flickering
I'd read out of the wavering
as flame, congealed

till what was then revealed
as a huge moon, began its rise
to be a second marvel, a moon that large & orange,
complete,
            contained—

then the familiar
diminishment & paling as it rode
higher, that ache
asking some participation that its shape
refuses, a lonely
circle, where the poem begins.

DAVID BROMIGE

"HOLD, HOLD"

We lay still
        our two worlds
laced as hands
when you said "look"
and we watched a mouse begin
a strange descent
along the piping to the lamp.

We could tell by the way
he paused
to close his eyes as if
pain took him in his gut
that he had taken
poison we'd set out.

               Naked
I rose and fetched a pail
a lead pipe
        nudged him into it
started to bear him out
when you said "maybe
you should drown him."
              It was
kindness to fill the pail with water
watching his fur go sleek
as he tried the slick sides
not a sound as he paddled
all of it held in the black eyes
not even looking at me
             but deeper into
the swirl of all things

and then I held him under
with pipe against the side
small bubbles
rising feet jerking
a spot of blood issuing
from his nose
              and myself held
in the steel sides
our chalice brimming with ripples going out
into shivering grass
the trees bending away
birds suddenly flying back
hawk in a plummet
                  its strings
cut

and all that night the stars
wheeled angrily like motes
in a muddied spring
              where I am
getting in deeper
in deeper in
deeper.

T. ALAN BROUGHTON

OF DANCING

My dancing is, in my opinion, good,
In the right, cramped circumstances, and provided
Other people are too preoccupied with
Their own to notice mine. I am happy
To have lived into an informal age when
Standing and shaking in approximate rhythm, not
Bowing and guiding, is the idea. Because to
Have to know regulated steps and be skilful was what
I could never manage at all when it was the thing.

So I do dance. But I'm never entirely sure.
It's a kind of movement you would never make
In the normal course, and how much it always seems
To obtrude on the natural in an embarrassing
Way wherever people get it started!
Set it apart, on a stage, with a large
Orchestra, it's all right, it's undoubtedly clever,
And the costumes are glorious to gawp at, but
It still looks a little bit foolish, moving like *that?*

To speak of how all its origins are so
Utterly primal—the planets, the seasons,
The rhythms of mating, and so on, and so on,
Is to list a lot of fundamental things,
Explain them, and exorcise dancing:
Because simply why dance if you've come to understand
What dancing mimes so roughly, or makes such
A repetitive pantomime of? Sleights of courtship,
Postures of delight, grief, vanity, idolatry I see

All around me more sharp and subtle for not being
Done in a style. Dancing has social uses,
I know, but so did elemental spears and punches before
They invented tables for eating and conducting
Verbal negotiation (and does hands
Gripping slyly under a table ever happen
In the middle of a fandango?)
Moreover, if the elemental stuff
Of dancing is banal, the ancient, ritual and customary

Panoply of 'the dance' is incredibly peculiar:
Fellows in feathers, or kilts, or puma-skins,
Guys trinkling little bells down there in Hampshire,
Or folding arms over black boots flicking in the
Urals . . . one surely turns away to find somewhere quieter,
Where one needn't be part of a silly circle
Of grins, clapping hands in moronic unison (I once
Took a pocket torch in, to go on reading—the *Listener*,
I believe—all the way through a Gene Kelly musical.)

For ostensible moralist reasons, the
Puritans disliked dancing; but they also
Opposed all giving and wearing of jewellery,
In which they may well have been right; so, with dancing,
They may also have come at the truth
From a wrong, religious direction. But, down Oxford Street
These days, whatever the mortgage rate, there jogs
In shine or rain an irrelevant group of chanters
Shuffling to the rhythm of tiny cymbals, opposing

Shaven sublimity to the big, crude, selling
Metropolis around; and *dancing*, in sandals, for converts.
They'd like to see everyone join them . . . how unlikely,
I think; and how such unlikelihood shows
That most of us only don or discard our
Finery, to dance, in a fit of social desperation.
I recall that outside the Hammersmith Palais,
There was once an illuminated sign announcing
A group of performers known as THE SANDS OF TIME.

For months, the words, I surmised, were a motto
Of that establishment: a thousand grains shaken
Nightly in that vast box, a thousand softies
Sifting for life-partners as the hours and days
Ticked on in tawdry, implacable rhythms. Yet the
Dancing prospers—telling how many the world leaves
Despoiled of words, of gestures diverse and specific,
Of shades of forehead, or hintings of finger-tips,
Or any more delicate tremor that speaks the whole thing;

And this is the crux. Tides vary, exact shelvings
Of pebbles on shores don't repeat, while patterns of clouds
Are never the same, are never *patterns*. Raindrops,
At unforeseen moments run, and weigh, down, minutely,
A million particular grass-blades: movement, movement,
Everlastingly novel shifts of a universe not
Gracelessly ordered, not presided by a setter of
Regulations. Vanity is so sad pretending to represent
Nature with humans dancing. Those who can move need not
    dance.

ALAN BROWNJOHN

IN OTHER PEOPLE'S HOUSES

In other people's houses
I pick up shells from coffee tables,
examine book titles,
take down fat volumes on calligraphy or Zen,
and thin ones by poets;
examine photographs, stones, Ming trees
and small Buddhas;
read anything in print,
such as bulletin boards,
fine writing on a
Sister Corita poster,
or a market list:
    (veal, watercress, toilet paper, Lux).
In general,
I ignore furniture unless
it is very bad
or very old;
paintings (unless Oriental);
flower arrangements (except dried grasses);
and anything on four legs,
unless
it is a cat.
If left alone,
my eye finds silver,
brass, and sometimes pewter,
and will select a window
if it frames water or a tree.
In other people's houses
I move between
clear and clouded surfaces·
I make do
with what I love.

JEAN BURDEN

SILENT JACK

My Uncle Johnnie, known as Silent Jack,
Suffered, despite his name, no special lack
Of words ; just kept them growling in his skull,
Jerking their tails, or lying half-awake
Till, without warning, like some starving back-
Yard greyhound one would scud out for the kill
—Frayed flesh, torn fur—or else to chase a joke
Around the bar until it burst, and bled
Under Jack's marble eye.   Then dropped down dead.

At Uncle Johnnie's house I'd watch him take
His dinner sitting by the red-tongued grate.
Self-banished, cracking fingers stiff as thorn,
He'd gently breathe a safe and separate air.
Unseen by others, prick my huge, child's stare
With a sharp wink ; penal, in socks, and sworn
By pomegranate-faced aunts not to swear,
And then, when the fouled clock struck ten past one,
He and his swag of walling-tools had gone.

I heard his drenched voice waver through the park
An 'Onward Christian Soldiers' at the dark ;
Thumps on the black-tarred door.   Aunts spiked the way.
'You're frightening the boy.' I hoped he'd stay,
For all the time I knew it was a play.
But, seeing me, he stopped, and turned, and fled,
And when an orchard apple sniped his head,
Thought it a shot ; died in the dry field-drain
But resurrected with the day again.

In eighty years he never ventured far
Past Sevenstones, but for Lord Kitchener :
Scarecrowed in khaki, kitted out with rum,
Puttees unrolled like Tablets of the Law.
They tried to teach him how to shoot the Hun,
But fighting was an art not Uncle John's.
Came first, they said, in the Retreat from Mons,
And all his country scholarship revived
In bloody situations ; and survived.

Though now he's underneath this hump of grass
And named and numbered on the written brass,
I see him slowly wiping tine and blade,
Listening to a hot-cheeked boy who took
Geese not for swans, but ducks.   Jack let that pass ;
A healing smile·   'It's each man to his trade.'
Six-and-a-half worn words from Silent Jack :
Where all around his drystone speeches stand
Printed upon the strong page of the land.

CHARLES CAUSLEY

LADY

1
Your hands embarrass the sun
Radiating in a crow's feather
And you want to wear gloves?

Your hands ripen peaches
And make the rain talk to itself.
When you cup your hands over my ears
I hear the sea singing,
And you want to wear gloves!

Then wear these gloves I'm making
With the first finger from sunlight
Combed from your colt's mane,
The second from honey I've gathered
In the hills on your chest,
The third from behind your ears,
This scent of freshly plowed earth.
The fourth finger is the face
Of morning on your cheekbones.

The thumb? Easy!
I simply sift the moonlight
Ripening in your hair
And mix it with the wheat fields
Shining on your knees.

2
First you came like the wind
    in a child's hand and I stood
    with a child's mouth open.

Then you came like feathers
    falling between snowflakes
    and I stood
    with a tree's arms reaching.

Then you zeroed in like night bombers
  or bees circling a flower.
I knelt in terror, my ribs open,
  sending up searchlights.

Now you don't even knock.

I turn around in the market place
  and there's your hand in the walnuts.
I walk the dark streets and you follow
  disguised as winter wind
  blowing night against my neck.
I fall asleep and watch you
  pulling on your long boots.
I wash my face, reach for a towel,
  and your hands dry my face.

Your hands with the fragrance of almonds;
Your fingers like the ribs of a ship;

Your presence like eagle tracks,
  that neither come nor go.

3
I marvel at the magic
And mystery of your entrance
Into my flesh and bones.

How sweet your presence.
Lady, what fresh bread you are!

4
All birds land, but you never land.
All streams and rivers pour down and out
Until they lie still and deep in oceans.
But you never cease flowing in my blood!

5
You are not here.
Then why, for the last ten minutes,
Have I been brushing your hair?

6
Jesus walked on water.
Our spacemen jumped into the moon's eyes.
You dance around these rooms inside of me
And I hear your hands sleeping.

7
I want no name for this,
No words to fence you in.

I will never hear your same voice twice.
No matter how many lights I use
I will never search or discover
All that is in your rooms.

This is the miracle I love.
Liking hiking up the mountains,
I keep moving with the pull of the path
To discover what is beyond the trees
Or around the bend in your elbow.

JIM CILETTI

IN ATHENS, OHIO

That one theme, all those years,
what was it? *My God, they are dying*
all around me, all
around me dying. Why,

when the leaves waved from branches
like trout breathing
the swift current, could I feel only
the shudder of the long fall
from light, the crashing body blind
drunk with fear, tripped up at last
with both hands in its pockets?

Oh My Love, I have seen our cheekbones smashed
like deer on the highway,
their staring eyes having beheld too much
in the night
rushing down upon them.

And always it was myself
that was dying
all around me. Within my hands
the darkness slept and woke
like mad women in closets,
longing for the sun.

This morning, in Athens, Ohio,
gray-faced men hug parking meters to their chests
like time bombs.

Oh My Love, you are the other dream
I cannot remember. Help me
memorize the sound
of your voice, saying, *This
now is my theme· Now you are living
all around me, all around me* ∘
living.

WAYNE DODD

THE MASKMAKER

He has begun making masks
the almond seller says
he is mad for hanging paper
faces in the street

The orange leers at the gold
while the purple laughs
and the white stares
his guild has gone berserk
he sells inhuman shame
in the sun my almonds
hurt no one
the priest buys almonds
for the poor but he
will not touch the masks

The maskmaker laughs
paper faces shift on the wall

His stall is alive
with strange expressions
we have not seen such people
what does he dream of
that such tortures come to him
in the night what has the darkness
done to him that he gives in
to such urges

They torment one another
the almond seller says
the town knows they are only
paper yet they believe them evil
the children will no longer play
in the streets the paper faces
rise upon them from the darkness

He is obsessed with colors
like the bones of Cassia's fish
he will never become haunted
with almonds

The melon man needs a new mask
for his daughter
his only customer has grown
tired of this simple one
he wants an amethyst this time
with black lines
under the eyes and green
on the cheeks
then he will have a fine new face
for his daughter
one that laughs

The maskmaker puts on a mask
it has grown dark but the boats
do not turn back
the child with the lilac face
is dead
the masks fly down the street
in the wind boats wander
dazzled uncaptained
the melon man drowns from the seawall
the almond seller is consumed
in his burning orchards

The stall is wet and dark
the paper faces have broken
against each other their eyes
run into other eyes
mouths melt onto the streets
they look up and see nothing
are nothing but so many colors

Listen as they pull
the maskmaker's bones from his body
and throw his flesh to the sea
which fills the cavities of skin
with its watery spine
the yellow mask walks
toward America

RUTH DOTY

THE GIRAFFE

Not one more animal, someone said, not one more—
And I agreed, having put a padlock on my private zoo,
When there was the delicate, left-out giraffe peering through
    the door.

I had to give in, I had to yield, I had to laugh—
One cannot leave out anything, one simply cannot:
If you do, you'll find the shingles of your house, in lieu
    of leaves, attracting the giraffe.

This demoiselle with a neck so long it sways
Lets her hobbled body crumple forward as it moves,
Too thin at the same time that her style is cramped by stays.

Go up to the second story, look the elongated darling in the face,
Tell her life is short and art is very, very long,
And, lacking elevator shoes to love her, you have, alas, not acted
    altogether in good grace.

It is good for art and even better for the soul
To climb up where the left-out have to look
And wear forever their tender, alienated faces on a pole.

No doubt the door cannot always be kept open, just in hope, just
    by chance,
Yet nothing but good can come of a quick, redemptive trip upstairs
For the high and lonely view of those who must conduct on stilts
    their version of romance.

CHARLES EDWARD EATON

THE SUN HELMET

The construction worker with the glistening hair
Is supple as a plant in all his thoughts,
Watering himself secretly with sweat.
His helmet, colored like a daffodil,
Takes and turns away the sun's hard kiss.
There's iron in this garden and deep, damp roots;
In the metallic light, a dipperful
Of water satisfies like jungle rain.

The structure rises but it cannot delve;
It is light rising from the worker's hand.
One block upon another mocks the glare,
The sun fights back as it has done
Since Babylon. Only a plantlike man
Can insinuate his secret power—
A passing cloud, and one remembers caves,
How the brain simmered paintings on the wall.

Under the yellow helmet, the head cools
A little, but the torso's rivers run—
What is the mix of solid, soluble?
Enormous blistering days and deep, dark nights
Contend along the narrowest catwalk,
The helmet arbitrates how high we go—
Without sun, no one ever would take heart,
A little darkness keeps the soul alive.

CHARLES EDWARD EATON

LOVE ON THE UNDERGROUND

'Are you sitting opposite
The new man in your life?'

Or is it that because of the people
Strap-hanging between, you cannot see
The man who is sitting opposite and
Would have been the new man in your life?

Can it be that you are not sitting opposite
The man who would have been the new man
In your life because he failed to fight
His way onto the train at the last station?

Is neither of you sitting opposite anyone
And is your heel digging into the sensitive
Instep of the person who will never be,
Not now, the new man in your life?

Or is the person who could have been
The new man in your life, is he
About to strangle the life out of you
Because you are crushing him to death?

We would not ask such difficult questions
Of innocent and well-meaning computers
Were it not that they have offered
To answer our difficult questions.

D. J. ENRIGHT

THE MUSEUM: THE PRISON: THE MADHOUSE

in some long still dance of pain
you come to me
in a stone ship, your name undone
to pictures on the prow:
the lion, the hawk, musician of the court

you stare at me with your blank eyes
and hold one hand   free
waiting for the falcon to descend
or a blessing to bracelet it
litanies for suicides & priests

though I cover the mirrors
you are everywhere before me
in the leaf   vein   cup
of my hands, in the weathered stone
with its face of human grief

in this last asylum you turn
& turn again, bringing feathers & harps of bone
in this dream my lover, in this a death—
the delicate choosings; murder, prayer—
we are both dead beneath our masks

yet in this last we run
like the fallow deer
through the mist on the glass, the briar,
in the mouth of the wind, the wind month
where only the gulls are crying

KATHY EPLING

WHY THE ENGLISH LESSONS ENDED

My Muslim neighbour's daughter,
getting on to nineteen
but not yet matriculate,
wears a *burqua* when she leaves for school
a hundred yards away.

They've tried and tried
to get her married off,
but three successive years
the girl has failed in English.
Each time the father railed,

the mother fainted, fasted and abused,
then they thought of me, the English Teacher
just next door. A little help
is all she needs, if you don't mind,
you know we are neighbours long long time.

I agree we are neighbours long long time.
Send the girl along, I'll see
what I can do. She comes, sheds her *burqua*:
tall, thin, dark, with shifting eyes, small face
and heavy clouds of hair.

She's very serious—for ten minutes,
then she smiles and smiles some more.
In half an hour she giggles. I learn,
giggling is what she's really good at,
with plenty of practice, not at home.

Friendly with my daughter
who's getting on to sixteen
and about to matriculate—
we haven't tried to get *her* married off—
she takes her home one day

and shows her pictures
in a certain kind of book.
My daughter tells my wife
who tells my mother
who tells me. I laugh it off.

She comes again, and suddenly
she knows I know. The English lessons
end abruptly. I've learnt enough, she claims.
(She's learnt enough to say she's learnt enough.)
The father rails, the mother fasts and abuses

but she will not resume.
They probably decide I made advances,
and almost hint as much
to my poor mother, who is outraged.
There's gratitude for you, she says.

That girl will never get a husband!

A month later she was married.
Now she doesn't need that picture-book.

NISSIM EZEKIEL

LET THIS CUP KEEP

Now let me cup my hands and hold the sun
between my palms as though it were your face
I kept. The touch is warm. The shape agrees
with plane and curve I knew. I think the bone
within the round of air. I think the man,
the flesh. I think I feel the past, and press
too hard. I break the cup I make. I lose
the light it bound. The light lies spilled upon
the earth. I stand in it. I let it lie
around me large as I would have your love
take place. You fill the wind. I breathe your breath.
You keep me, and I call my life the day,
You deepen, and I live the night. I live
in time a bowl you cup my being with.

NORMA FARBER

THE WAY SHADOWS REFUSE

Flat on the street
they may be lying
angled to their tree

or pole. They may look
lifeless, two-dimensioned
replicas, dull, dark,

compared to the original
uprights on the tree-lawn.
Not steadfast. Not real.

But watch the way
those shadows refuse to be run
over! They rise up and waylay

cars, buses, ambulances—
throwing their non-weight
around whatever body runs

between them and the root
of their being. They embrace
hood, chassis, trunk, with a great

crooked clasp. They press their sign
on the least intercepting child.
When he's gone they lie down.

NORMA FARBER

PRISON ISLAND

That's the Naples packet slipping out of the harbour
With a fat Bourbon guard and a hold full of capers
So perhaps my letter will have escaped the censors.
But I have no news· What change could there possibly be
Except that the rats have got at the Indian figs

Water is low again and the trip I was planning
Across the jagged headland to explore the next cove
Has been forbidden.   How are we supposed to survive
On these dry terraces, under a haze but no cloud ?
Summer has even deprived us of our wider view.

We think we are in a great ocean miles from our homes.
Then one morning, waking after a trivial storm,
We find the curtains lifted and the panorama
Temptingly displayed once more.   The sea becomes a lake
Whose farthest shore is Sicily where the native towns

Of my defeated friends pursue their normal business.
Beneath the coast a sail suddenly catches the wind
And becomes visible—a tan sail on a grey ship.
I wish that I had never heard these people's music
Which burdens the mind with the gloom of false memory

Making me dream recently of going home to you.
The city gate was locked but I walked through noiselessly
Along the colonnades.   It was dark.   Shutters contained
All that was left of conversation in the houses.
The bright conspirators were dead with their feeble jokes

And sat still at the tables of the artists' cafe
In their old attitudes, one with his arms stretched outwards
Encompassing a point that was lethally untrue.
There in the doorway, caught tossing his cloak for effect,
Stood the bringer of bad news whom none of us believed.

I walked on, hoping perhaps to find you still awake,
And turning by the town hall came into a new square.
Wooden scaffolding still enclosed the triumphal arch
But the vast galleries were open to the moonlight
And the smug granite facings were gleamingly polished.

An equestrian statue provided the focus—
Though not for the nightwatchman playing cards by its plinth.
Summoning my courage I approached them to enquire
In whose honour all these renovations had been made.
The guards ignored me.   I realised I too was dead.

My dear friend, do you value the counsels of dead men ?
I should say this.   Fear defeat.   Keep it before your minds
As much as victory.   Defeat at the hands of friends,
Defeat in the plans of your confident generals.
Fear the kerchiefed captain who does not think he can die.

New prisoners bring news.   The evening air unravels
The friendly scents from fruit-trees, creepers and trellised vines.
In airless room conversations are gently renewed.
An optimist licking his finger detects a breeze
And I begin to ignore the insidious voice

Which insists in whispers : The chance once lost is life lost
For the idea, for the losers and for their dead
Whose memorials will never be honoured or built
Until they and those they have betrayed are forgotten—
Not this year, not next year, not in your time.

JAMES FENTON

TWENTY YEARS OF HEARING JACK

while adjusting the Victoria Cross i laugh
her concern away my grandmother is ill: the reality
of her eventual absence touches me as i touch
her tissue thin skin lift her wispy hair to fasten
the clasp: today is the anniversary of jack's death
in the war she's telling me now i stop laughing
wonder if he died speechless & woudn't have had
anything to say to her either but lift wispy hair
:   this is how we begin with tissue thin skin
like an embryo you can see through
while adjusting the Victoria Cross i laugh
her concern away—her eyes search my face worriedly
she gives me a paper napkin says Diane you & your
    poems

i run
wild as the candelabra strawberry feelers
stretching over the brown country earth
from memories that were not mine down
broken sidewalks chunked out raised
over poplar tree roots last trees to lose
their leaves beyond war time photographs
yellowed drawn from dusty drawers

jack
who carried a photograph
of me as a child

i straighten the Victoria Cross
on the bulging bone of the old breast
its weight is a ton
in my hands & a feather
on her tissue thin skin

DIANE ELIZABETH FRY

THE BATS

Somebody said for killing one
you got a five-dollar reward
from Red Farrell the game warden,
because at night they drank cow blood,
dozens of them plastered on the cow
like leaves after a rain
until she dropped.
If they bit you you'd get paralyzed for life,
and they built their nests
in women's hair, secreting goo
so you couldn't pull them out
and had to shave it off.
That was how Margaret Smith got bald,
though some said it was wine.
But who ever saw one,
or could tell a bat from the swifts
they sometimes flew with,
homing on insects those green evenings?
We never climbed the fence of Duffy's orchard
to catch them dog-toothed
sucking on his pears,
and the trouble was, as Duffy always said,
that in the dark you couldn't
recognize them for the leaves
and might reach up and get bit.
So the first time one of us found one
dead and held it open,
it looked like something crucified
to a busted umbrella,
the ribbed wings a crackpot inventor might make
to try and fly off of a dune.

As if it was made up of parts
of different animals, it had long bird-legs
stuck in lizard-wrinkle pants,
and wire feet.
It wasn't even black, but brown and furry
with a puppy nose,
and when we threw it at each other
it wouldn't stick on anyone.
Then someone said his father knew somebody
who used to hunt between town and the back shore.
Coming home one night he ran across
a bat tree in the woods,
must have been hundreds folded upside down
pealing their single bell-notes through the dark.

BRENDAN GALVIN

THE DROWNED CHILDREN

You see, they have no judgment.
So it is natural that they should drown,
first the ice taking them in,
and then, all winter, their wool scarves
floating behind them as they sink
until at last they are quiet.
And the pond lifts them in its manifold dark arms.

But death must come to them differently
so close to the beginning.
As though they had always been
blind and weightless. Therefore
the rest is dreamed:
the lamp, the good white cloth that covered the table,
their bodies.

And yet they hear the names they used
like lures slipping over the pond:
*What are you waiting for,
come home, come home, lost
in the waters, blue and permanent.*

Louise Glück

THE LADY KNIFE-THROWER

In the gay silver air of the tent
I'm at ease, fingers
at rest in my lap.
Before me the tools of my trade—
cleaned, well oiled, and waiting
for the warmth of my hand, for the time
when the flick of my wrist will send them
out into the morning for their casual trip
to my husband's waiting body.
One at a time, they plant themselves at his sides,
tucking in the air around his body.

At night, under the big top,
he is strapped to the board.
With a roll of drums I appear with my knives
and release my repertoire of throws.

There is no question in our lives of fidelity.
At night, after the knives are cleaned and placed
in their teakwood rack, we are all we desire.

DANIEL HALPERN

CARNAL KNOWLEDGE II

Grasshoppers click and whirr.
Stones grow in the field.
Autumnal warmth is sealed
in a gold skin of light
on darkness plunging down
to earth's black molten core.

Earth has no more to yield.
Her blond grasses are dry.
  Nestling my cheek against
  the hollow of your thigh
  I lay cockeyed with love
  in the most literal sense.

Your eyes, kingfisher blue.
This was the season, this
the light, the halcyon air.
Our window framed this place.
If there were music here,
insectile, abstract, bare,

it would bless no human ear.
Shadows lie with the stones.
Bury our hearts, perhaps
they'll strike it rich in earth's
black marrow, crack, take root,
bring forth vines, blossom, fruit.

  Roses knocked on the glass.
  Wine like a running stream
  no evil spell could cross
  flowed round the house of touch.
God grant me drunkenness
if this is sober knowledge,

song to melt sea and sky
apart, and lift these hills
from the shadow of what was,
and roll them back, and lie
in naked ignorance
in the hollow of your thigh.

GWEN HARWOOD

GRAVE

Look! how that neglected grave
thinking itself alive and all things other dead
brings forth thanksgivings of daisies,
sweetbrier and wild strawberries
and tenderly lays them on the air.

RAYMOND HENRI

THIS FATHER OF MINE

*I want to show you something
very beautiful,* I say to my father
in this dream. We are walking
a tar road in Nesconset

around a slow bend
I still remember
where elms rose up
every evening of every summer

into great forests of darkness,
and blue-black birds swept
from one branch to another.
I want to show you something

very beautiful, I say, and take him
by his hand that never held
a book, his palm hardened
by boards and the handles

of a hundred hammers.
I notice sawdust
in the hair on his forearm.
I want to show you something

very beautiful. Now,
past the road's pebble and sand shoulder,
we step into oakbrush
where a path winds downward

to a pond I still remember.
In this dream the pond,
as it once was, is lipped
by ferns mirroring themselves

in green triangles
all along its edge.
On the far shore
a crane beats up out of the water,

curves over the trees,
hangs suspended
on its white wings
as though it were the white moon climbing

motionless in time
for as long as we stare. But
*I want to show you something
very beautiful,* I say to him,

and now, somehow, at the end
of the path of this dream,
we are barefoot, wading out
to knee-high water where

the pond's bottom disappears
into a depth I still remember.
There, I say to him,
and point down.   But

from his pocket
he takes a handkerchief,
and stands, this father of mine,
knee-high in water in no hurry

wiping his glasses.
Over the far shore
the white crane still flies
to nowhere, motionless

as the white moon.   But
there, I say, and point down, and now, at last,
we are looking down again
into the dream together,

into the pond's deepest beginnings,
into the place I remember
where elms rise toward surface
from the black water, from

thousands of fathoms, each leaf
distinct, each trunk furrowed
black and deep as a field
of plowed loam. *There*:

fish swim in the branches and bark valleys,
blue-black carp that vanish
and appear, and vanish again,
and appear. Their gills

glow red, their tails seem
to spray wakes of pale
yellow arcs as the fish vanish,
and appear, and vanish again, and appear.

Yes, he says, *yes,* and now
as though from his one word
spoken into the darkness of this dream,
the carp scatter

downward and outward
forever. And now that I have held
our two worlds together
for as long as this, the day,

in the whitest light we have ever seen,
rises from the bottom of the water through the elms.
It is over, I think,
though I almost remember

that we hold hands again,
and talk for the first time,
and walk toward home,
which is far away.

WILLIAM HEYEN

A THIN TIME

A thin time. The world hesitates
With timid bud pricks, in the spiky hedges
Littered with newsprint rags and plastic scraps.
You are gloomy, and we tramp a marly lane,
Round by a shabby wood, across a plough.
I am fascinated by its frothy tilth,
Primed for the seed, its clean soft harrowedness

In this delicate surface of its nothingness
A hillside of wheaten substance soon will rise.
The sun draws at it already, in the ground.
The copses seem to be waiting, waiting to smell again,
Want to be active with the huzz of summer.

Nothing grows between us: I try to kiss you
But it is unwelcome. Our depression settles
On the dun old grass, on the dead
Shrivelled blackberry relics of last year,
A summer we did not know. Nor shall we
Know this good bramble here this season.

Moving house, and the ensuing homeless panic,
Uncovers to us a deeper blank perspective—
The well-cleaned earth that bears no relics of us.

When we are gone, and the house gone, the harrow
Passes over, and the green blade thrives in summer.
Where are our imprints? The little press
Of your unwilling cold cheek on my lips is gone.
Our figures in the bare March landscape whizz
Into the great grey mist of an Anglian sky.

Tea-time comforts us, in from the desert,
Shuts out the great grey fields of not-being:
Five small blue candles on a remnant of Tom's cake:
I light them, his five years: bright, they flutter,
Like gassy moths, and then so quickly,
Thinly burn out. Ten times as many
Would waste as rapidly. In desperation
Your smile breaks out at me. Dust under our feet,
Our waxy calculations flicker into smoke:

A thin love-line now binds across the chasm
Like the drill-marks on the fields, where, in the hedges
We found the guide-marks, thin white scraps in cleft sticks.

DAVID HOLBROOK

BURNING LEAVES

In Memory of Mark Van Doren

They tended a cold November fire in a field
    And watched. There was nothing to say. There were
The duodecimos of summer being burned,
    Old, damaged greenbacks consumed, to give way
Not soon but soon enough to a new currency.
    The poem of burning needed no title.
And if one muttered, "How hungry fire is" and if
    The other took the mild reminder for
A teaching, it was not drawn from any teaching
    Of the leaves, burning in the wind, imbued
In their reddish or tan pallor with a touch of
    Consummation. For there was no hunger
Of fire like that of light, frail skeletons of leaf
    Famishing for altitude now that so
Little was left. But rather, as they raked at the
    Gray ashes with their gaze, uncovering
Here and there protesting tongues of flame and under
    Everything the hot, silent ember heart,
Steadfast, rather were their decipherings of fire.
    They were like the smallest girl in a group
Of four who stares at the yet unlit pyramid
    Of autumn leaves the others still heap up
As if at present flame, and like them unaware
    That a paling sequence of poplars shrinks
And fades into the dark ground in the cold of a
    Perfectly painted twilight behind them.

What, then, of the readings of leaves? Barren or green,
    Their brief flights are not theirs, but of the winds.

A careless girl in a rocky cave leaves her door
    Aflap in the gale: her journal's pages
Scatter and lie piecemeal; their only messages
    Are of their own dispersal, and the stray
Albumblatt someone pressed and framed, while legible
    Is trivial. Nor is one ever to
Come upon a huge form seated in a dark glade
    Turning over leaves of leaf, pages in
The Book of Leaves—to come upon him and perhaps
    To read in the tremblings of his hidden
Lips, and in the rustlings of his beard, the very
    First versions, the earliest folios.
Thus for the two in Northern Connecticut who
    Watched the slow burning of the summer's bones
There was mere meditation: their faces opaque
    With thought, smoked with remembrances, they
        stood
Attending rising ghosts—but only of the leaves,
    Which, yearning to rise, finally can go up
Only in smoke. Naturalists, they eyed the flecks
    Of ash and gasps of spark. Pastoralists
Of old song, they brooded over where burning went,
    While above them the flakes of morning mist,
Invisibly radiant with information,
    Dispersed, clouded with the disturbances
Of smoke that they made and stood watching being
    made
    In a dying bonfire of deadened leaves.
Americanists of the air, they inhaled there
    The difficulties of dissolution,
And heard breathing the impatient signifiers—
    Consuming heat, the eaten leaves, and food
For thought as smoke becomes part of the sky—pressing
    For recognition. Far away, it goes
Without saying, there lay, under a clear sky whose
    Blue remained rinsed of all perplexities,
A gray stone house by an unreflecting, chilled lake
    Ringed about southward by the laughing Alps.

JOHN HOLLANDER

IN THE MOON-BACKED MORNING

In the moon-backed morning and the bunting light
how soon our bones have bent and burnt,
though our cheeks hold fast to the wind's slack
and our kites still chase each other up the slope,
though the lamp of my breast has blown out,
and the well of your childhood tears is spilt.

How we hide from the stony world, hide-and-go-seek
and run-sheep-run! Yet still where the earth is green
we can run out again, still where the earth is cold
as its chalk and slate we can play ghosts, still
where the earth begins at the bird's blind cliff
we can fly unafraid, yet in the stone's built town we shake.

Not desert nor famine rode us to such a street,
nor did the riding ills of childhood's diamond light
sail us faint. Flood did not ride us to the wall's
shack-raft, nor did the breaking weathervane
wheel all directions wrecked. The stork laid us
down to our whipped and seersucker garments.

Yet when the flooring moon to the stork's stone town
is swept, see how our arms light up with bones.
We hear the lighted wagon of childhood drawn
rattling its toys toward radium and the clocking room.
Look at our transport, how building blocks mix with broken
dolls, the ceramic arms and the stone's tears unlocked.

Now in the devolved and seeded house, by radium watch,
our bones' bright slope reels to the seabirds' coast
in the twinkling air, and the wishbone thighs
lie still, but the eyes' blue air is whole,
and starred in the bunting morning light from dark.
At the breast's burnt lamp such bright bones are burning.

And still so bright the stork who snowed us down
to our priestly frocks and nursing room, who told
by its wedded wings our appointed saints, who told
in ringing weather how to run our blowing kites
once the snow was broken and we were born together.
Twin, in the moon-backed morning unfold, remember.

ORA MAY HULL

CINDERELLA LIBERATED

I sleep with
my feet in the fire
destroying the evidence
one glass shoe
melting like butter
both feet black as briquettes
while the prince
in a world of questions
searches for an answer
he carries near his jewelled sword
the other shoe of the pair
he drinks from it champagne
or Schlitz and that's not
all he does he has
a special pillow for it on his
bed where he polishes it
and in it sees his own
reflection
it has become his talisman his illusion
his astigmatism and his lotus
let no man touch it it's
all he has left
that and this note
dear sir whenever you see
rising from the ashes a bird its feet
blazing like torches
observe closely
it passes for me

ANNE HUSSEY

OCTOBER 1973

Last night I dreamed I ran through the streets of New York.
Looking for help for you, Nicanor.
But my few friends who are rich or influential
were temporarily absent from their penthouses or hotel suites.
They had gone to the opera, or flown for the weekend to Bermuda.
At last I found one or two of them at home,
preparing for social engagements;
absently smiling, as they tried on gown after gown
until heaps of rich, beautiful fabric were strewn
over the chairs and sofas. They posed before mirrors,
with their diamonds and trinkets and floor-length furs.
Smiling at me from the mirror, they vaguely promised help.
They became distracted—by constantly ringing phones,
by obsequious secretaries, bustling in with packages,
flowers, messages, all the paraphernalia,
all part of the uninterruptable rounds of the rich.
The nice rich, smiling soothingly, as they touched their hair
or picked up their phone extensions.
Absently patting my arm, they smiled, "It will be all right."

Dusk fell on the city as I ran, naked, weeping, into the streets.
I ran to the home of Barbara, my friend,
Who, as a young girl, rescued four Loyalist soldiers
from a Spanish prison;
in her teen-age sweater set and saddle shoes, knee socks,
she drove an old car sagging with Loyalist pamphlets
across the Pyrenees all the way to Paris without being caught.
And not long ago, she helped save a group of Basques
from Franco's sentence of death.

In my dream, Barbara telephones Barcelona.
I realize this isn't quite right,
but I just stand there paralyzed, as one does in dreams.
Then, dimly, from the other end of the line,
through the chatter of international operators,
we hear artillery fire, the faint tones of lost men,

cracked voices singing "Los Cuatros Generales"
   through the pulsations
of the great, twisted cable under the ocean
Agonía, agonía, sueño, fermente y sueño.
Este es el mundo, amigo, agonía, agonía.

"No, Barbara!" I scream. "We are not back there.
That's the old revolution. Call up the new one."
Though I know that, every day,
your friends, Nicanor, telephone Santiago,
where the number rings and rings and rings
With never an answer. And now the rings
are turning into knells:
The church bells of Santiago
Tolling the funeral of Neruda, his poems looted,
His autobiography stolen, his books desecrated
in his house on Isla Negra.
And among the smashed glass, the broken furniture,
his desk overturned, the ruined books strewn over the floor,
lie the great floral wreaths from the Swedish academy,
the wreaths from Paris, South Asia, the whole world over.
And the bells toll on . . .
Then I tell Barbara to hang up the phone.

She dials the number again, then turns to me, smiling,
Smiling like an angel:
"He is there." Trembling, I take the phone from her,
And hear your voice, Nicanor,
sad, humorous, infinitely disillusioned,
infinitely consoling:
"Dear Carolyn . . . " It *is* Nicanor!
And the connection is broken, because I wake up,
In this white room, in this white silence,
               in this backwater of silence
on this Isla Blanca:
               Nicanor, Nicanor,
are you, too, silent, under the earth?
               Brother, Brother.

CAROLYN KIZER

ICARUS FLYING

It is one kind of madness to try always
To gauge how far from the sun you are,
To hold a course just without its heat.
To keep that imaginary line which dips and lifts
Is as impossible as to catch up from the beginning
The measure of what is love and what, passion.
Your wings would wet, grow heavy
In the indifferently smiling spray of waves
Which sing for no-one, not even for you.
You would stumble into the sea
Like an awkward young osprey
Which has not judged the span
That separates the sea and rocks.

It is another kind to see that you fly too close,
To know suddenly, before the feathers spin down,
The perfection of the random paths they must take.
Too late you would find the balance,
Discover the gift of all tongues was yours
To approve those wings worked
With the care of a calligrapher for each letter.
You would watch the wax with which your life was sealed
Break, like great sluggish clots of blood, and drop.
You would fall and love with the sureness
Of an artist's eye your height from the green water.

In the one there is only fear.
In the other there is fear and time
Enough to utter what is sweetness
In the form of your death.

Susu Knight

EMBLEM

(poem for July 1)

Up to my waist in water
trying to open a culvert
blocked by beavers intent on
flooding my bottom fields

I ram and ram a cedar pole into the plug
until with a great wet sucking sound
the walled up water bursts through.

I am blowing hard   sweating
welted by mosquitos and black flies.
I am also mad.   The third time this month.

The brown water   green-speckled by pollen
rushes from the opened culvert
carrying wattles and mud
of how many beaver hours and miles.

No use being smug.

They are sitting in the weeds   waiting
for me to head up the spongy lane
they'd soon have made impassable.

All night while I try to sleep
they'll chew and tote and pad and pat
and by Wednesday next   all the lodge brothers
will gather to slap broad tails and smile.

But what the hell   that's the way it should be;
once they were currency and survived debasement.
They were here first and I should know it.

I'll have to negotiate for every inch I get
and maybe wind up with a real good beaver pond
and a bridge.
We should all be so stubborn.

CALVIN LAPP

SHEET MONGER, BLANKET HOARDER

Sheet-monger, blanket-hoarder,
wool gatherer of nightmares,
wrapped in white linen like a corpse,
wrapped in your dreams, a strait-jacket,
I remember that night in Frisco
when we got our new bodies.
It wasn't an operation
performed by a team of specialists;
it wasn't a heart transplant;
nothing was sewn or grafted.
In our new bodies it was a miracle.

And all those years beaten by love,
strangled by love, crazy in the head for love,
you thought you were dying.
Your body, you were sure, was dead
like a person in trance, far away,
but you wore it to remind yourself—
a woman dressed in black.

I, too, was much the same,
at forty-five, pot-bellied,
throwing the dirt in my face,
dirt from the grave,
the undertaker's hand on my shoulder.
I dreamed of the breasts
and thighs of young girls;
I stood before the mirror
as at a wake,
long hair, loud shirt and loud slacks;
at least I would go in style.

Then we got our new bodies.
Your hand touched my arm
and my face, a death mask, was clean;
all the dirt fell away, a truckload.
And the young girls died instead.
Your hand touched my arm
and you stood there in a white dress
like a woman after a bath. And you were beautiful.

Sheet-monger, blanket-hoarder,
small-breasted Annie, my skinny, my love,
the night we got our new bodies
we threw all the covers off.

Philip Legler

REUNION

Your son has betrayed you,
he has decided to become a god.
He leaves home to join the organization.
You don't see him for years.

You meet him finally by chance
in the dead of winter,
a hitchhiker you pick up
on the way to the hockey game.
He is not yet a god.

You drive him through icy streets
to the workshop where, he tells you,
the organization has sent him,
to learn how to make
useful artefacts out of clay.

He is taller than you remember,
his voice softer yet more disciplined.
He speaks of his inner peace,
but you don't listen closely.

You are intensely aware of the cold.
It must be ten below
and the heater isn't working.
You find it hard to believe
it is your son beside you.
"Soon I will be a god," he says.

The workshop is boarded up,
but there are several people inside.
When you go through the door,
a young man with gray hair
and a hawk's face
says something to your son,
who picks up a small dish
and smashes it on the concrete floor.

The other man nods approval
and turns away.

"I think you'd better leave,"
your son says.
And you say that you love him,
knowing it will be your last chance.

LAWRENCE MATHEWS

IN MEMORY OF W. H. AUDEN

1

His heart made a last fist.
The language has used him
well and passed him through.
We get what he collected.
The magpie shines, burns
in the face of the polished stone.

2

His was a mind alive by a pure greed
for reading, for the book
which "is a mirror,"
as Lichtenberg said: "if an ass
peers into it, you can't expect
an apostle to look out."

It was a mediating mind.
There were the crowds like fields of waving wheat
and there was the Rilkean fire
he didn't like
at the bottom of the night.
He loomed back and forth.
The space shrank.
The dogs of Europe wolved
about the house,
darks defining a campfire.

3
My friend said Auden died
because his face
invaded his body.
Under the joke is a myth—
we invent our faces:
the best suffer most and it shows.
But what about the face
crumpled by a drunk's Buick?
Or Auden's
face in its fugue of photographs
so suddenly resolved?
It isn't suffering that eats us.

4
They were not painting about suffering,
the Old Masters. Not the human heart but
Brueghel turns the plowman away
for compositional reasons
and smooths the waters for a ship he made
expensive and delicate.
The sun is implied by how
the sure hand makes the light fall
as long as we watch the painting.
The sure hand is cruel.

WILLIAM MATTHEWS

I THINK MY MOTHER NEVER KNEW

I think my mother never knew,
Through all their shared and tender years,
What made my father lie awake,
Or half of what the man went through;
Except that all his private fears
Were borne for someone else's sake.

It was no fault of hers; he kept
To himself whatever plagued him; so
Lying awake at night was just
His chance to work things out. If he slept
Or not, he never let her know.
His silence she would take on trust.

Why did he do it? I think I see
The way he saw it; something about
If you have problems, only you
Can find out where the balm might be;
And if you still can't work things out
There's no use asking others to.

I suppose in this moaning age
A man might be described as quaint
Who shouldered trouble silently.
But I respect my heritage,
In which no self-absorbed complaint
Could ever conquer dignity.

Perhaps he was the loser; though
Leaving us all in health could be
Enough to make the man content.
And it would please him, could he know
His wife, alone, sleeps easily,
And lives on what he might have spent.

ERIC MILLWARD

BEING A SOLDIER (FOREST HILLS)

for Stan Smith

It must be to have hair beneath the arms,
must be at the conclusion of the set
to leap across the net wearing success
as though it were familiar and accustomed,

the face it seems the face one always wore,
the perspiration knifing down the back,
the regulation shirt stained, body-clinging.
It must be to be young, it must be winning.

It must be lying evenings in the barracks
being indistinguishable from the others,
in underwear with one's name stenciled on it
listening to the guitar six cots down,

to be stationed near Indianapolis
or somewhere equally removed from water
where twilight takes a long time in the cornfields
and the girls order milk shakes at the drive-ins.

In the sun it must be to come to power,
to move as though such endless barracks waiting,
nights sweet with June, July, seem not excessive
if in time it means it may come to this:

last-minute drives unerring in their timing,
leaning into returns with crucial skill,
impeccable the intricate half-volleys,
slowing the serves to thwart a rival's forehand.

It must be to lie back in Pasadena
(that California of the life or mind)
examining the trophies on a shelf
where the last half-light kindles little fires

in the depth of the bowls of golden cups
or rages through the cool rows of medallions
where silver waits to be touched by that life.
It must be to be twenty-four and blond.

Sipping champagne sent by the racket maker,
"The army has been good to me," one mutters,
one hears oneself explaining to reporters,
forgetting the anonymous guitars,

not mentioning the nights of barracks waiting,
the suns such long time going down, the golden
girls drinking butterscotch milk shakes at the drive-ins,
those Indianas severed from the sea.

It must be to go home and, like the rest,
to lie alone at evening, to be dreaming
hammering cross-court, playing into darkness
no evening falls sufficient to bring down,

a wind raking the ankles, private's sweat
whose salt-lash eats the lips, dreaming two wrists
dazzling enough to light one through that life
where night, like justice, inundates the courts.

HERBERT MORRIS

THE DISAPPEARANCE

Take the Arlo Guthrie records with you
Take the hotels we built on Marvin Gardens

In the Volkswagen drive until the night
tells you what to do with your life

Were you, too, one of those players
knew Boardwalk wasn't worth the anguish
waiting always for someone to land
knew the yellow each time around
could be hit for something substantial

In the Volkswagen drive until the night
shows you what to do with the night

We can wait, most of us, a lifetime
for such instruction, players half as
beautiful as you are or were
seated some night across from us
someone willing to risk it all
as we advance around the board
and are positioned on, say, red
ready to move as chance determines

The one for whom this poem is written
the one for whom loss is a magic
pawns the hotels, half-price, on purple
mortgages railroads, sells Park Place
surrenders what must be surrendered
does all but take bids on the silver
all but let fifties fall to knees
browned by the sun weekends this summer
all but promise that for two thousand
she'll sleep tonight with you, the banker

merely to build on green on green
merely to hold within those hands
whose depth I hesitate to state
yet struggle not to overstate

the power to annihilate you
should your leap not exceed her grasp
should the dice bring you to Pacific
like a raft with a doom-bound sail
convert you to the taste of drowning

We can wait, most of us, a lifetime
to feel, to find, somewhere be found
like the girl in that masterwork
of the Italian cinema
who, in time, eluded them all
who so successfully escaped them
defied their deepest expedition
that sweep of isle, that scan of sea
that inconclusive penetration
that, by mid-course, the major burden
had shifted from the thing they sought
to that life together as seekers

In the Volkswagen drive until the night
lends a shape to the evening, says the night
as Arlo Guthrie shall not have recorded

Deep in hotels we built for Marvin Gardens
on the sheet of the bed in the last suite
lining that corridor of wind and salt
on the top floor, facing the sea, east wing
think of the granules of blond sand collecting

We shall wait, most of us, a lifetime

In the Volkswagen take with you
all that you need to live that life

the newest album of A. Guthrie
snacks for the journey, for the desert
water for the American drought
the deed, of course, to Marvin Gardens
those hands, which I cannot imagine
scattered on points between the night
and the routes south to desolation

finally, in a clear glass vial
always in view lashed to the dashboard
grains of a dazzling tawny sand
gathered slowly from cracks and floorboards
of an old bleached summer hotel
stars for a roof, moonlight for sheets
beached in the bracken of Pacific
or should you own as well the yellow
making that corner treacherous
going down somewhere in the wastes
of a dry, dusty, failed Atlantic

HERBERT MORRIS

DEPARTURE

Where have you gone, ferrying north
To Kenai, hoping?
The ranges have swallowed you, one by one,
And the time of our knowing fades.
Where have you gone, ferrying north,
While the tide brings gifts to my feet?
Always dead fish ride in the air
And my friends, the clouds, come to sit.
News from the south is late, as usual,
And strange from those centers of fury.
Oh why did you go, ferrying north
Up the inlet of dream and desertion?
The salmon run small this year
And the cold continues.
Oh why did you go, ferrying north,
When time was yet to be?
Oh why did you go, ferrying north,
When ours was a harvest, waiting?

SHEILA B. NICKERSON

BARN OWL

Ernie Morgan found him, a small
Fur mitten inexplicably upright,
And hissing like a treble kettle
Beneath the tree he'd fallen from.
His bright eye frightened Ernie,
Who popped a rusty bucket over him
And ran for us. We kept him
In a backyard shed, perched
On the rung of a broken deck-chair,
Its canvas faded to his down's biscuit.
Men from the pits, their own childhood
Spent waste in the crippling earth,
Held him gently, brought him mice
From the wealth of our riddled tenements,
Saw that we understood his tenderness,
His tiny body under its puffed quilt,
Then left us alone. We called him Snowy.

He was never clumsy. He flew
From the first like a skilled moth,
Sifting the air with feathers,
Floating it softly to the place he wanted.
At dusk he'd stir, preen, stand
At the window-ledge, fly. It was
A catching of the heart to see him go.
Six months we kept him, saw him
Grow beautiful in a way each thought
His own knowledge. One afternoon,
Home with pretended illness, I watched him
Leave. It was daylight. He lifted slowly
Over the Hughes's roof, his cream face calm,
And never came back. I saw this;
And tell it for the first time,
Having wanted to keep his mystery.

And would not say it now, but that
This morning, walking in Slindon woods
Before the sun, I found a barn owl
Dead in the rusty bracken.
He was not clumsy in his death,
His wings folded decently to him,
His plumes, unruffled orange,
Bore flawlessly their delicate patterning.
With a stick I turned him, not
Wishing to touch his feathery stiffness.
There was neither blood nor wound on him,
But for the savaged foot a scavenger
Had ripped. I saw the sinews.
I could have skewered them out
Like a common fowl's. Moving away
I was oppressed by him, thinking
Confusedly that down the generations
Of air this death was Snowy's
Emblematic messenger, that I should know
The meaning of it, the dead barn owl.

LESLIE NORRIS

THE GRAVEROBBER'S CHILDREN

We are the children of the graverobbers.
Our eyes have been sewn shut,
our pale lids
crossed with a needle of catgut.
We can't see
the chopper rising from its nest of rags,
the gas wings beating after rat fur.
Still we see
shadows of the dead
roving in the boiled egg of the brain,
the ghost germs
breeding light on the back of the beast.
Our mouths have been stitched up,
our blue lips
laced with coils of spider silk,
drawn tight past the point of trembling.
We can't sing
the beauty of the bullet
biting into the baby's heart,
murdering the image in our mother's blood.
Still we sing
in whispers of the drowned,
mosquitos murmur at the root of the tongue.
We've been forbidden
music as well.
Our ears have been plugged,
our soft ears
stopped up with wads of sealing wax.
We can't hear
the crow's cries,
the prayer breaking from the neck of the hung.
Still we hear
rain crawling in the trees,
the soaked branches brushing the stone slabs.
We can't move.

Our limbs have been chained down,
our frail hands
bound to the ground with batwing webbing.
Still we stir
when the stars fall,
the earth shudders under the ferns,
our fingers dance on the tips of the moss.
We can't eat—
our sweet-tooth is gone.
Light-years ago we ate something too sweet,
they denied us our dinner.
A cadaver drinks
from the same stream,
the innocent fish wince in the water.
Still we feed
on the moth dust, we gobble the mold,
we stuff ourselves piggy with mushroom spores.
And famished
we thrive on the corpse crumbs,
the left-overs.
Our nails grow, our hair rises,
we've outgrown our hand-me-down coffins.
Other children are free
to run in the fields with flame in their hair,
dreaming of milk;
but we are the children they have killed before.
This figure of fire
burns longer in our bones
than a crib-full of toys ablaze on our birthday.
And nightly they come,
the hooded ones—
with their burlap sacks, their instruments,
the precious stones hidden like candy.
Again and again,
as the wolf calls, the moon darkens,
our fathers come to tempt us to their trade.

ILMARS PURENS

FREE FALL

In the year 1900, a French tailor proposed to fly from the top of the Eiffel Tower in a robe he had himself devised and made. Film cameras recorded the experiment.

A long while, a long long while it seems:
The bat-winged figure shaking his robe,
    The cameras purring.
It is Daedalus the tailor, up on the Eiffel Tower
Ready to fly. The year is 1900;
    We watch it now.
. . . Shakes at his bat-robe, first to the right,
Then left, then right again, a twitch,
    A doubtful gesture.

"Cast thyself from the pinnacle, angels will bear thee up."
So great a height—the wings will surely beat
    And bear me up?

Shaking his robe. A mile of film we are wasting:
Why doesn't he jump? In these long seconds
    What is he thinking?

That the plan was crazy, and the careful stitches
Shaped him a shroud? Perhaps he is wondering
    How to withdraw,

To pretend a flaw in the work, a change in the wind;
And imagines how it would be to face
    The jeering crowd,

Slink back to his trade and live, with nothing to live for.
So still he hesitates, and shakes his shroud,
    Then, suddenly jumps.

Not even a flap from the wings. The lens below
Can barely follow the plummeting shape,
 So quick his fall,

Hollowing out his own grave.
We are caught between dismay and laughter
 Watching it now—

Not in a myth, not a century back, but now.
Ridiculous death. Yet as he stood on the tower,
 Shaking, shaking his robe,

He mimed what each man must in private try,
Poised on the parapet of darkness—
 Each in that crowd, and you, reader, and I.

ANNE RIDLER

SILENCE AND SPEECH

1
My birth was lonely. I had not made friends.
I could not speak the language of the place.
When troubled by an enigmatic face,
I did not know an empty smile transcends
A doubtful thought. A normal child pretends
That everything is right. But in my case
I did not trust the food. In time and space
My story almost stops before it ends.

In space, I stretched myself. It was in spite
Of pre-existing blobs that circled me,
Ingesting particles of form and light.
In time, I made my shape and day. I see
The white mist rise to meet the falling white:
I practice, in these woods, my mystery.

2
Are there some lives that open painlessly
Like paper toys you drop in water? They thought
I was an idiot: never to be taught
To walk, to talk, to clean myself and be
A franchised outlet of humanity.
I watched them from my silence, and I caught
Their mournful look: what changeling had they got?
With a wild rending, I gave birth to me.

I search at this late time without despair
Internal woods. I'll call you on the phone
Next week and tell you if the secret lair
The Truth-Beast keeps is lost or overgrown.
The mist has gone. The snow falls everywhere.
The self I made knows how to be alone.

3

The synthesis I made was overthrown
When someone died. No other death had torn
The fabric thus since I was doubly born.
I did not think my life could be resewn.
She was a woman and a light that shone
Into my darkness. They wanted me to mourn
By their convention. I wanted to unlearn
Myself and drop through water like a stone.

I stand here by the window and occlude
The sunlight. It will never be again.
I lived through the obscenity of food,
Obscenely hating each live citizen,
But now her love pervades me; quietude
Is not despair—she chose me among men.

RALPH ROBIN

YEAR OF THE MONKEY

Night with a Veteran Winter, 1968

1

She sleeps and he imagines her asleep
in the next room
She sleeps and with her few words
dreams out loud among warm animals
false in the terror of darkness should she wake

She sleeps easily
now that her father who was gone
is home
He cannot sleep tonight

Restlessly he stares against his hands
hears wind in trees
the stealth of wind
tries to think it coaxes grass
from ground scorched by dry snow
here where there was snow

No snow where he has been

Fire and the smell of fire

2

Late in a bright room
all the shades drawn, door locked
careful to keep his shadow
from betraying him against the shade
he listens
hears a car rip thin strips from the wet street
hears them tear up rags for bandages
sees the strange face bending down to his face
feels the breath
the blast

dim bodies near him smouldering
the reek of sulphur
bodies still as dolls

He feels the reaching hands
touch him as he disappears

Then the noise of newspapers wrapped around a wound
a thousand wounds
crowded
into darkness weeping without shame
more than he can comprehend
as he stares at his own healing hands

He wakes again
to the nightmare waking
where a figure wrapped in paper
in the next bed stares
Again he watches
helpless
as characters he cannot understand
blur with a sudden stain
and the wide-eyed man is dead again

3
Outside the branches barb with buds
The wind slips through
house after house unheard
moves from room to room
enters each sleeper, pauses
then moves across the lawns
between the houses of the neighbors sleeping
while in their dark garages
corrupting with the rust of steel-salt
cars hunch like unfinished tanks

While they sleep
and wind blows endlessly across their sleep
across a continent asleep
he listens

If he drew the shade, threw the window open
shouted
some of the sleepers nearest him would stir
and whimper
dream of someone crying
Fire! Fire!

But their sleep is undisturbed
his wife's sleep is unbroken
He knows what his hands mean
their groping in the darkness
their wooden stupor when he wakes
from dreams of bodies still as dolls
and he knows he'll endure it all

4
It's late and he is tired
He shifts
to let his shadow lapse across the shade
and waits, trembling
Nothing
no sound but the wind
his own slow breathing

The strange face bending down to his face
and he sleeps
but dreams a dream of fire
he won't remember when he wakes
nor this crying out

The child hears him, stirs
the wound reopens

The stain spreads uncontrollably

WILLIAM PITT ROOT

TALKING MYSELF TO SLEEP IN THE MOUNTAINS

Longing, I have seen you in the water
Flare like a bluefish in your native place.
You are at sea level, dark-headed lover,
Twelve hundred miles of night southeast of here.
I have come up to thirteen hundred feet.
Hammer is with me, fly rod banging
On his shoulder as we clambered uphill
Sweaty with friendship, lying about the South.
We crossed the wind-burned ridgeback wild with berries,
Spooking and being rattled by a doe
In that dry cover, hiking up our packs
And skidding sideways to this run of water,
And the thick trunks smoking up the moon's half-light,
Tall poplar, beech—and saplings for the tent.
Now in the darkness we have pitched our camp.
Clear as it is, the creek will not pool deep
Enough to carry trout, so we fish out
Two cups of stone-cold water, bank the fire,
Bite down on that and whiskey on the tongue.
The fire is smokeless and the talk is good
And sifting into nothing like the fire.
The moon is blurred when I climb down to shiver
In the creek again and watch the light
Through stone-chinks stammer like a dream toward dawn.
Hammer is snoring when I climb back up.
This is a good place, it would be good
To sleep here with you and to bathe downstream
In the pool we are bound to find tomorrow.
It could happen. You could come here with me.
But I am laying on this going fire
The maps of every likely place I've been
For light enough to get back down to you.

GIBBONS RUARK

LOVE POEM

1

Who could take another spring
like this, the starlings
nesting in the pines like black
fruit, the dark blood
of the grass beginning to flow
again, the white stars
of the snow digging their graves
in the sea of mud.

2

The flowerbeds are swollen with water.
The drainpipes overflow with leaves
and twigs, the bodies of small insects
are sliding down the shingles.
The slow rain is everywhere.

3

Yesterday my wife took off
her clothes for the first time
in a week. The light
from her body glowed like the red
lamp of the darkroom. When I touched her
breasts I could see my bones
shining through the cups of the palms.
Her eyes were like pockets
of midnight, her stare went through me
like a tongue of black secrets. What sun
could fly through the body
like this, what rain, which dark birds?

IRA SADOFF

MADNESS

I used to believe that nobody was really crazy,
That people were all basically good. Sometimes it was
A question of coaxing them, a little, but in the end
You'd get back what you gave and more even.

But as I grew older I learned that's not always the case.
You have evil in this world as you have anything else.
I remember the first time I noticed someone was crazy.
It wasn't interesting, really; I only wanted to leave

And go someplace else. There was nothing to discuss.
The fact is it was boring. I had no impulse to make
          myself
Clear because that isn't possible—there was no inter-
Action at all; nothing but the rushing noise of a bird

Trying to escape a cage, its wing sticking out, or its head,
But never its whole self. The talk is self-obsessed.
Being inside the cage has made it a sudden stranger to
          the air,
And whatever appears in it. But the cage is not there

At all. There is only a person, one who looks deceptively
Like you or me, except for a certain deadness
          —recognizable,
After a while—in the eyes. If you spend any time at all
You notice a tendency to repeat, the mind is trapped in a

Vicious circle, trying to make itself supreme over
Everything by accepting nothing but its own hysteria.
It would be sad, I suppose, except that it is uglier
          than that.
You find yourself looking away, after awhile, and when
          you

Look again—you find the same thing. It goes on and on.
It has nothing to do with you. It has nothing to do
     with anybody,
Not even the person there in front of you. They are
     possessed,
Not by their own bodies, but by the evil that is very much

Part of this world. They are weak—or they were, I guess,
Before the evil entered them. Why else would they let
     it in?
But once it happens they acquire the power of what has
Entered them, the power of evil. I believe this power

Is of no small consequence, as witness the evil of this
     world.
But I believe the power of good is of greater force, in
     the end.
The man who makes himself the vehicle of the power
     of good
Causes the man of evil to become envious and finally
     suicidal.

ARAM SAROYAN

104

BECAUSE

Because
I cannot quite manage
The over-loaded grocery cart
The snow-suited baby
The little boy
And the awkwardness
Of the child within,

I say to him
That he must watch the cart and baby
Just till I bring the car

And
Seeing the small white face
In the headlights

I know this must be how it begins
For all the women who cannot quite manage
And all the children left to wait
In supermarket lots.

BARBARA SAUNDERS

IN THE AIR

It's a hunter's moon, red
as dead coral. Tonight we counted—
we lost count—of the hours.
The reeds have closed around the pool.
The pool has lost all record of our catch:

three trout we have brought home
in shallow water, wondering
at the thirst they felt as air
began to stiffen them with little gulps
in the pail that sloshed to our pace.

By the trailing hooks we lift them out,
silver as pale tubers, silver-green,
and slimed with tendril weeds.
As the gritty water lets them go
they feel the night along their swallow bodies,

their mouths become stiff ovals in the air.
You flap them flat on the ground.
Their painless eyes gaze on the scene of death:
this, then, is the air, and these its creatures;
here there is no grace in how things move,

and the dead do not float up
gently to the surface and lie still.
—You clean them with a knife.
You chafe the tiny coins into the pail.
You gut and lay them out beside their bones.

The eyes don't notice what they look upon.
We wear the silver, and the moon has found
a thousand burning mirrors on our wrists.
The scales stick. Our hands are fish in water
where they touch. We draw them up like roots.

MICHAEL SCHMIDT

LETTER FROM BROOKLYN

"Mrs. Rosen," thirty years ago a
warden of a Nazi extermination camp,
was recently recognized by two of
her former prisoners, in New York,
and subsequently arrested.

Thirty years
I've lived here safely, but
Today a look of recognition

Stopped me dead, as if
Out of the corner of my eye
I'd seen shoes sticking out

From beneath the drapes, as if rolling
Over in bed, I'd seen a spy
Instead of clothes on hangers.

I know that woman, all of them, they say
"He vanished so fast . . . the water
Was left running. Upstairs, footsteps

Scattered like dropped silverware.
We fled like roaches." So did I,
I changed my name to Rosen, dyed my hair,

Yet recognition spread, a bruise
Across her face. Whispers
Seep under my door like gas. What now?

A porcupine in a taxidermist's box,
For every needle on my back
A murdered Jew. She lifted the lid and shined

A flashlight on my terror—
I'm stuffed, packed away
In sawdust, but today she saw
The pupils of my marble eyes contract.

GJERTRUD SCHNACKENBERG

STORIES OF MY MOTHER'S CHILDHOOD, TOLD IN WARTIME

From the album of my mother's mind,
Secret in their innocence,
The dead walked out in comic hats
To posture in a new pretence.

My uncles, always young and smart,
In Norfolk jackets cut the hay,
And Granny in a long white frock,
Tripped abroad to gather may.

Embowered in abundant peace,
The farm where all the Farrs were born
Rose tranquilly amid its flocks
Its blossom trees and golden corn.

The winters of the war were cold.
The people hid in smelly lairs.
But we hid out in Gloucestershire,
In a cupboard underneath the stairs.

I knew we'd have it all one day,
Just as Grandpa meant we should.
We'd feed the hens, and milk the cows
And go for picnics in the wood.

I didn't know that Grandpa drank
Till his cattle and crops had rotted black,
And the boys went off to die in France
And the burden broke old Granny's back.

And yet my mother never lied
And gave me more than half a fact.
She shared with me the charity
That keeps a dignity intact.

MARGARET SCOTT

MOTHER

While we slept our mother
moved furniture.

Through our dull unfocussed
dreams we could hear
the coarse scrape
of chairs and the sharp sound
of her breath easing
the sofa in place, its plush girth
opening fresh wounds
in the wallpaper.

In the morning we found
the amazing corners   startled by pure
circuits of light we'd never
seen before, pleasing
elbows of space and new shapes
to fit into   bringing us
closer to rebirth
than we ever
came   in all those years.

CAROL SHIELDS

SERVICE CALL

His van arrived
witty as a rooster—
he had come to repair
our troubled telephone.

From the window
we watched him race
leather-haunched up
the serious pole

and there
leaning alone
into green-wired leaves
buzzing with gossip

he phoned from an oval
of space
pure perfect numbers
we'll never know.

CAROL SHIELDS

THE OWL ON THE AERIAL

Just at dusk
As the full moon rose
And filled his canyon,
Out of his crevice
Floated the owl,
His down-edged wings
Silent as moonlight.

With three-foot wingspread,
Claws that could paralyze
Rabbit or squirrel,
He battened on beetles
Drawn to the manlight,
And just for a little
He lit on the aerial,
His curved claws clutching
The shining metal.

Softly the moonlight
Sheened on his feathers
While under his feet,
Unfelt by him,
The moon lay still
And men like those
In the house below
Floated upon it.

CLARICE SHORT

HE MAKES A HOUSE CALL

Six, seven years ago
when you began to begin to faint
I painted your leg with iodine

threaded the artery
with the needle and then the tube
pumped your heart with dye enough

to see the valve
almost closed with stone.
We were both under pressure.

Today, in your garden,
kneeling under the sticky fig tree
for tomatoes

I keep remembering your blood.
Seven, it was. I was just
beginning to learn the heart

inside out.
Afterward, your surgery
and the precise valve of steel

and plastic that still pops and clicks
inside like a ping-pong ball.
I should try

chewing tobacco sometime
if only to see how it tastes.
There is a trace of it at the corner

of your leathery smile
which insists that I see inside
the house: someone named Bill I'm supposed

to know; the royal plastic soldier
whose body fills with whiskey
and marches on a music box

How Dry I Am;
the illuminated 3-D Christ who turns
into Mary from different angles;

the watery basement,
the pills you take, the ivy
that may grow around the ceiling

if it must. Here, you
are in charge—of figs, beans,
tomatoes, life.

At the hospital, a thousand times
I have heard your heart valve open, close.
I know how clumsy it is.

But health is whatever works
and for as long. I keep thinking
of seven years without a faint

on my way to the car
loaded, loaded with vegetables,
I keep thinking of seven years ago

when you bled in my hands like a saint.

JOHN STONE

EXORCISM

No mourning for the unborn.
Rabbit in the snare
Trout on the blind hook
Shad in the weir
Buck in the rifle-sight
Grieve me more.

Eggs cold in the nest
Are caviar of the gods.
All meager weanlings
Parched, greedy chits
Comfortless weepers
Trouble me more.

Ghost of the unborn,
Importunate impostor,
Babe of a barren mother,
Old stones teach me
Grief's for the living.
Haunt me no more.

CONSTANCE URDANG

TRANSFORMATIONS

At night a green ring is humming,
a circle dipping between pines,
singing over a floor of needles;
it moves, a litany of insects,
in praise of full July.

By day, leaning there in dry grass,
you stretch out your hand;
you see wide wings on stalks,
wider wings in air.
They pause in the heat for you,
waiting for dark, knowing you will come.
The noon-air splits
with your coming, no illusion.

Till the earth warms roots, and you,
till the sun drops and a green ring rises,
you will stand like a trunk, immobile;
but they find you, and ring you,
and give you their shape and their light
till *you* are the shape of the month,
the clay and needles and sap,
the stalks and cups at noon,
even the luminous wings.

Cory Wade

THE LESSON

That promising morning,
Driving beside the river,
I saw twin newborn lambs
Still in a daze
At the grassy sunlight;
Beyond them, a day-old colt
As light-hoofed as the mare
That swayed over his muzzle—
Three staggering new lives
Above the fingerlings
From a thousand salmon nests—
And I sang on the logging road
Uphill for miles, then came
To a fresh two thousand acres
Of a familiar forest
Clear-cut and left for dead
By sawtoothed Weyerhaeuser.

I haunted those gray ruins
For hours, listening to nothing,
Being haunted in return
By vacancy, vacancy,
Till I grew as gray as stumps
Cut down to size. They drove me
Uphill, steeper and steeper,
Thinking: the salmon will die
In gill nets and crude oil,
The colt be broken and broken,
And the lambs leap to their slaughter.

I found myself in a rage
Two-thirds up Haystack Mountain
Being buzzed and ricochetted
By a metallic whir
That jerked me back toward life
Among young firs and cedars—
By a rufous hummingbird
Exulting in wild dives
For a mate perched out of sight
And cackling over and over,
Making me crouch and cringe
In his fiery honor.

DAVID WAGONER

LIVING IN THE RUINS

The tyranny of doors swung shut and bolted
Against a knock or the scratching darkness
Has ended with these breaks in your walls
Where anything may leave or enter
As the moon and the wind decide. The ceiling
Has settled comfortably across the floor;
The stairways have faltered
Like waterfalls whose careless water
Is falling as far as all split-level living
To its logical conclusion in rubble.

Lean at a window now and feel no longing
For all that lay out of reach: it will reach you
Simply, uncalled-for, here in this open season,
And you must take what comes to your windowsill
To make itself at home, while broken glass
Blooms where the iris was.

What happens naturally is the advent of moss
Turning these stones to sand, establishing
The separation of powers with its rootless searching.
You have nothing to be coveted but your life:
Tending a fire to make your share of the weather
And living in these ruins to reconnoitre
Your strangest neighbor: night falling around you.

DAVID WAGONER

TALKING TO BARR CREEK

Under the peachleaf willows, alders, and choke cherries,
By coltsfoot, devil's club, sweet-after-death,
And bittersweet nightshade,
Like a fool, I sit here talking to you, begging a favor,
A lesson as hard and long as your bed of stones
To hold me together.
At first, thinking of you, my mind slid down life a leaf
From source to mouth, as if you were only one
Piece of yourself at a time,
As if you were nowhere but here or there, nothing but now,
One place, one measure. But you are all at once,
Beginning through ending.
What man could look at you all day and not be a beggar?
How could he take his eyes at their face-value?
How could his body
Bear its dead weight? Grant me your endless, ungrudging impulse
Forward, the lavishness of your light movements,
Your constant inconstancy,
Your leaping and shallowing, your stretches of black and amber,
Bluing and whitening, your long-drawn wearing away,
Your sudden stillness.
From the mountain lake ten miles uphill to the broad river,
Teach me your spirit, going yet staying, being
Born, vanishing, enduring.

DAVID WAGONER

VIPERS,

sliding, pour themselves through themselves,
bits of miniature rivers.

Slack else, still
as worry beads left where they fell,

they abrade the young year's sun
in grit, green, brick, stucco brown,

a crumble. Always the eyes, coppery red—
sometimes the tongue, loose threads

flickering the wind.
This one I found

dead today, coils in a coil,
fills its Chinese bowl

with spent resilience. I'll keep it
as long as this takes to write.

Never before did I own a viper. Touch,
flinch,

to remember dry heaths of boyhood
summer, brackens, the sandy birchwood,

yelping in a pack for the hated snake—
deadly adder. With a fork-ended stick

you'd fix his wriggling, knife his
sin. It was the lore of boys:

make a belt of the skin, heat
the flesh in an iron pan for the fat

that cures deafness.
Older, with a first girl in the sharp, dark grass,

you listened for the swift sibilance
of adders, appalled; and appalled in the silence

after, still you'd listen.
But, since, you've seen them often,

commonplace on an afternoon path,
exotic, arcane, tempting as death

to disturb. Several, zigzagged, ravelled as whips
lashed round themselves, whirls and loops,

finally subsided, a muddled tie-drawer.
One, disentangling, sloughed like a whore

peeling a stocking back. The new
head, mint as a pebble damped with dew,

had to be smashed. This one that's mine,
stiff in its small blood, its venom mine

for the simple milking, could kill
from posthumous spite. Did Adam, some residual

innocence left him in his great age,
lift the serpent's carcass in homage

to the nighthawk?
In the garden, to the dark

under the rose arbor, I commit this thing,
watched from the window. The fang

feels like red wire. I'd have
let this one live.

TED WALKER

THE UNEMPLOYMENT INSURANCE COMMISSION
POEMS: 1. THE NATIONALIST

I know you, countrymen.
I have lived here my whole life.
I know your nature.   If the Reds
should swarm out of Asia
or earlier still the imperial
Japanese had set foot in
Esquimalt, how you would fight!
If they imposed on us
so horrible a government
that hundreds of thousands of us
had no work, were promised
compensation, and retraining for jobs to come
and then this was forgotten
or given in dribbles or
lost in the filing system
between one desk and another
—the nation would rise.
The middle class
would stop reading novels
and join the thick-fingered carpenters
in the most secret of underground cells.
No one would watch TV for a week.
Everyone would arm themselves
at the newest outrage
the sports page would die
of loneliness, lecturers would give up
preparing material on
Comic Books and the Canadian Soul
poets cease looking at
histories of animal stories
for proof that Canadians side
with the weak, and the beaten.

What riots there would be, my countrymen.
What slogans appearing by night.
What murderous and continual gunfire
and strikes to turn a whole city
into a snowstorm of fear.

Ah, but when it is not an invader
but your own people
who condemn you to a lifetime of sand:
what a heaviness is here.
To be assured that the money is yours
that you are entitled to the money, and so
to plan for the money, to need it
to go somewhere warm, out of the cold
without the tedious and embittered
asking of friends.
To know that you don't have to worry
that you *have* the money.
And then to have the money never arrive.
To be told to come back Friday
and on Friday to come back Monday
and on Monday to wait
until Friday's mail, and on Friday to phone in
Monday to see and on Monday to come in
for an interview Friday.
To be informed by print-out
that you do not have enough weeks
when you have enough weeks.
What is there to do now?   Now
you must wait
until the phone is free, until
the line moves up another man
until your case can be re-opened
until they locate your file
until you can get another appointment.
And in the meantime
ask them what you should eat.

"Sand," is what they say.
"Open your window and eat sand.
Scoop what you can live on
out of the passing air."

Now you know what it means not to have a country.

TOM WAYMAN

SOFTSHOE

All you need is a white room
and a good long shoe with a certain flap
and a kimboed looseness in your squatter.
Tricky knees might help.

A white room like silence,
all the furniture out,
one room like that—tall and cold.

Look in the mirror behind you
and see the little gent in the baggy suit
pick up the rhythm, go swinging with the whiteness
around the room, as though it was his.

He knows the movement of the prophecies,
the swat and switch, the spin of stick
and hook, the heft of whiteness.

If I could do that
I would give up loving women,
I would quit the whirl of whiskey
and the imminence of snow.

So I will go out and drink—
carry eagles out, and a little music
until my heart is free and movement fluid.
I have been thinking
all my life about dancing.

ROBERT LEWIS WEEKS